2ND EDITION

WRITING GREAT BOOKS for YOUNG ADULTS

EVERYTHING YOU NEED TO KNOW, FROM CRAFTING THE IDEA TO GETTING PUBLISHED

REGINA L. BROOKS

 sourcebooks

Published by Sourcebooks, Inc.
P.O. Box 4410, Naperville, Illinois 60567-4410
(630) 961-3900
Fax: (630) 961-2168
www.sourcebooks.com

Library of Congress Cataloging-in-Publication Data

Brooks, Regina.
  Writing great books for young adults : everything you need to know, from crafting the idea to getting published / Regina Brooks.
     page cm
  Includes index.
  (trade : alk. paper) 1. Young adult fiction—Authorship—Handbooks, manuals, etc. I. Title.
  PN3377.B76 2014
  808.06′8—dc23

                         2014017319

          Printed and bound in the United States of America.

                VP 10 9 8 7 6 5 4 3 2 1

To my late great-grandmother "Hannah," for whom the molding of young adults was a craft.

CONTENTS

INTRODUCTION

"Welcome to the world of Young Adult Fiction."

Those are the words I use to kick off the workshops I conduct at various writers conferences held throughout the United States and abroad. But they're not just words. If you want to write YA fiction, you've got to be willing to step into a whole new world.

This book is designed to help you enter that new world. Here you'll find detailed descriptions of how to avoid the traps many potential YA authors fall into, as well as tips on how to create the next YA bestseller.

WHAT IS YA FICTION?

Of course there are universal standards for writing prose for any audience. To a large extent, however, elements of YA fiction, especially the tone and the narrator's perspective, differ markedly and require a whole new set of rules.

This notion of YA's otherworldliness doesn't seem to be a concept understood by most people who want to write for teens, at least judging from the manuscripts that cross my desk. I hear similar comments from colleagues in the YA world. Most of these pros wouldn't be surprised to hear that among the stacks of manuscripts I receive, 90 percent of the writers seem confused about what YA fiction is.

It's not surprising that people are confused, given that something as basic as a list of bestselling YA titles is commonly found on the same page as picture books for toddlers, complete with lift-the-flap and pop-up features. The illusion of YA as solely an extension of traditional children's books may also explain why many novices who try their hand at writing for teens rely on memories of what they enjoyed reading in adolescence. Depending on the individual's age and experiences, that might mean nineteenth-century Louisa May Alcott's *Little Women*; J. D. Salinger's *Catcher in the Rye*, published in 1951; S. E. Hinton's *The Outsiders*, 1967; or Judy Blume's *Forever*, 1975. Highly commendable classics all, with messages that continue to resonate with youth, but they don't necessarily represent what YA editors are looking for now.

So what is YA fiction, exactly? Most publishing industry insiders consider YA fiction to be fiction written for readers from about the age of twelve to eighteen, featuring characters in that same age range. Keep in mind, however, that these age boundaries are somewhat flexible. While YA can often be a coming-of-age story, not every coming-of-age story is YA. If the character is an adult reflecting on his youth, that's not a YA novel.

As a literary agent representing writers of different genres, one of my jobs includes presenting my clients' manuscripts to editors who decide whether they will purchase them for their publishing houses. Editors develop areas of expertise, such as food, science, business, and religion. I have long noted that certain personalities gravitate toward YA publishing, and that they have sensibilities and interests that are strikingly different from editors who work in other genres.

Just as teens like to push the envelope, YA editors, who generally have easygoing personalities, are more open to taking risks. They are often willing to try fresh approaches and formats. It is this dynamism that makes them more experimental than button-down.

Mirroring their readership in another regard, YA editors exhibit high levels of curiosity. Most significantly, in addition to wanting to inform and entertain, they care about getting young people to read, and seem determined to publish books that address adolescent vulnerabilities and engage in the problems of the day.

None of this is meant to suggest that they should be nominated for sainthood. Like anyone else in business, editors must keep their eyes focused on the bottom line. Because that requirement doesn't seem to diminish YA editors' sense of purpose, it enhances the illusion that they inhabit a separate world.

The tremendous creative and commercial success of YA lit is improving opportunities for writers and readers, giving the genre the respect it deserves. Rick Margolis, executive editor of the *School Library Journal*, which he describes as "the largest reviewer of children's books in the country," points out that he does a lot of reading and believes YA books are now among the best genres being published across the board.

Agreeing with Margolis, Carol Fitzgerald, Book Report Network founder, whose company launched Teenreads.com in 1997, explains, "YA books are shorter than most of those written for adults. That requires authors to write with wit and precision." She says proof of their exceptional quality is in the fact that many YA books are winning awards traditionally won by adult fiction.

Among the increasing numbers of YA authors cited for excellence is M. T. Anderson, winner of the 2006 National Book Award for *The Astonishing Life of Octavian Nothing, Traitor to the Nation*. An exemplar of how writers can cut their own swaths through the YA world, Anderson employed multiple viewpoints as well as letters, newspaper clippings, and scientific papers to tell the story of Octavian, a black youth raised as a Revolutionary-era slave.

Anderson's story is one of many YA entries that will be discussed here in a chapter-by-chapter feature, "Anatomy Lessons," which includes advice and encouragement from award-winning authors. Another ongoing feature in this book is "Advice from Publishers Row," encapsulating wisdom from top YA editors. My intention is to give you the sense that you have a panel of experts standing at the ready to guide you through the writing process. One more chapter-by-chapter feature, "Author Working," will help get your creative juices flowing.

CROSSOVERS

A lot of people in the publishing industry believe that confusion about what constitutes YA lit is heightened by the success of some titles known in the industry as "crossovers." Publishing houses generate additional revenue from some books by marketing them to both adult and YA readers, thus crossing over from one audience to another. Francesca Lia Block's cult novel, *Weetzie Bat*, written in 1989, is considered the original crossover, continuing to attract readers from fifteen to thirty-five. Two of the most commercially successful crossovers are Mark Haddon's *The Curious Incident of the Dog in the Night-Time* and Yann Martel's *Life of Pi*. Both were published in 2002 and have sold over two million copies each. Those books were adult books that crossed over into the YA market, but there are others that start out as YA and then cross over to an adult audience; for example, Stephenie Meyer's *Twilight* series and Cecily von Ziegesar's *Gossip Girl* series. The first became a feature film and the second a popular television series. All these crossovers have led to the creation of a new genre, New Adult, which is the focus of Chapter 13.

Author of the crossover series Harry Potter, J. K. Rowling has said she had no particular age group in mind when she started *Harry Potter and the Sorcerer's Stone*; however, she did know she was writing for children. The first Harry Potter novel was eventually published in 1998 by Scholastic, the world's largest publisher and distributor of juvenile books. The company targeted *Harry Potter* to children nine to eleven. What happened, of course, made publishing history, with Rowling's work garnering millions of fans worldwide, both older and younger, including a substantial segment of teens. Later, two separate editions of *Harry Potter* were released, identical in text but with the cover artwork on one edition aimed at children and the other at adults.

Rowling's young wizard also cast magic on the YA world, changing the way the industry viewed the genre. *Harry Potter*'s $29.99 selling price reminded publishers that young people were not only willing to shell out big bucks to read but that they also had the means to do so. In 2006 in the United States alone, teens had $94.7 billion a year to spend, a figure that increases about $1 billion a year, according to Jupiter Research.

Rowling's success led to her books being turned into movies aimed squarely at teens, and again they attracted a much broader audience. The *Harry Potter* film series is on track to become the top-grossing franchise in movie history. The success of a book can often inspire producers to look at YA books specifically for the purpose of making movies aimed at teens. Some examples of book-to-film include *Twilight* by Stephenie Meyer; *Ella Enchanted* by Gail Carson Levine; *Confessions of a Teenage Drama Queen* by Dyan Sheldon; *I Know What You Did Last Summer* by Lois Duncan; *Sisterhood of the Traveling Pants* by Ann Brashares; *The Fault in Our Stars* by John Green; *The Hunger Games* by Suzanne Collins; *The Fifth Wave* by Rick Yancey; *The Book Thief* by Markus Zusak; *Divergent* by Veronica Roth; and *The Hitchhiker's Guide to the Galaxy* by Douglas Adams.

As I'm sure you've noticed, the market for YA film adaptations is huge; ten adaptations alone were made in 2013. These cinematic successes mean that YA books are reaching broader audiences than ever before—parents, film executives, and other adults. The numbers bear this idea out. According to *New York* magazine, the two biggest audiences for YA fiction are readers ages eighteen to twenty-nine, who buy 35 percent of all YA purchases, and readers ages thirty to forty-four, who buy 27 percent of all YA purchases. Similarly, these success of these film adaptations make the YA market look lucrative, spurring authors to write for it. The end result is that YA is a multimedia genre that transcends the page.

While many YA novels have crossed over into the adult market, that should not be the goal of your YA manuscript. Instead, focus on writing the best-written book you possibly can. Crossover audiences follow the best-written book, so producing an outstanding manuscript should always be your aim.

THE NEW WORLD OF YA FICTION

As my friend and editor Kat Brzozowski tells budding writers, "A lot of YA books do edgier stuff now. Teenagers' lives now aren't the same as they were twenty years ago."

Over the decades, teens have been changed by a combination of what some describe as less parenting and more media. The nation's wake-up call came in April 1999 when two boys went on a shooting rampage at Columbine High School outside Denver. Eric Harris and Dylan Klebold killed twelve classmates and a teacher, and wounded twenty-four others, before committing suicide. The massacre provoked a national debate about cliques and bullying.

Shortly after Columbine, Carol Fitzgerald, founder of the Book Report Network, spoke to a gathering of publishing executives. "I told them that compared to what's really going on in the lives of young people, the books that were being published read like pabulum. I reminded them that they owed more to young people and to their teachers and parents, and I asked them to give teens books that matter in their lives."

A lot of publishing executives must have had similar thoughts. A proliferation of titles followed that immersed readers in the real world. During the eighties and nineties, YA authors had tackled subjects such as premarital sex, homosexuality, and AIDS. But many books published in the new millennium delved into risqué subjects such as incest, drag queens, oral sex, self-mutilation, and date rape. Edgier and trendier, they are not your mother's storybooks, and maybe that's just the point, suggests Mark McVeigh, a senior editor at Dutton. He says, "The lives of kids today are barely recognizable from the childhoods anybody over thirty led in the way they approach sex, drugs, alcohol, parental attention or the lack thereof."

Keep in mind that teenagers live in the same world as you do. They don't live sixty years ago, they don't "go steady" anymore, and being asked to the upcoming sock hop is hardly the greatest of their concerns. One of the most important things you can do—in fact, one of the standards by which your novel will succeed or fail with its readers—is to accurately reflect the world and how today's teenagers perceive it.

LIVING THE DREAM

I assume that you picked up this book because you have something you want to communicate to today's teen readers. My goal is to help you understand and avoid the challenges and pitfalls of writing for today's YA audience.

Experience tells me that working through this book will not only help you produce a better manuscript but will also allow you to look at your own world with fresh eyes. That has certainly been the case for me. I started out with a degree in aerospace engineering from Ohio State University and as an avid reader was attracted to a career that lasted more than a decade in senior positions at major publishing houses like John Wiley & Sons and McGraw-Hill. While I still feel equally at home in the mathematical world of engineering as in the literary world, I have been able to creatively mine my technical background in helping writers hone their craft. Engineering trained me to identify areas of strength as well as structural weakness, and because that's what editors do, I have learned to think like an editor in evaluating manuscripts.

Because I'm in a profession that allows me to represent authors I deeply respect, I derive a great deal of pleasure from championing their work. An agent is an author's first line of defense. But we learn right away that in the business of writing, not everyone loves the same books. Sometimes it takes a while until a manuscript lands in the hands of just the right editor.

Keep that in mind as you learn from this book, developing your manuscript and polishing it like a gem before you hand it over to those who will judge it. My advice is that when possible, learn from criticism, but don't let it weigh you down. (I work with one writer who records any nasty criticism she receives on paper towels, which she then burns.)

It may help you to know that the author of one of the most famous YA books of our time was described by a critic as "not having a special perception or feeling which would lift the book above the curiosity level." *The Diary of a Young Girl*, first published in 1947, was written by Anne Frank, a gifted Jewish teenager who detailed her life in hiding in Nazi-occupied Amsterdam before she died of typhus in a prison camp. Later, First Lady Eleanor Roosevelt spoke for many of Frank's fans, describing the diary as "one of the wisest and most moving commentaries on war and its impact on human beings." Readers seemed to agree. The diary has sold more than twenty-five million copies.

Perhaps this story will help you remember that critics, much like the adolescents whom I hope will populate the pages of your new world, are only human. Also keep in mind that while every ear may not be sympathetic, most criticism is intended to help you create the best possible book you can. With that in mind, I hope you will grasp the tools contained in this book to produce your own *Catcher in* the Rye, *Harry Potter and the Half-Blood Prince*, or *Sisterhood of the Traveling Pants*. I, for one, look forward to reading—if not representing—them.

CHAPTER 1

FIVE RULES FOR ENGAGING READERS OF YOUNG ADULT FICTION

Before you even start putting pen to paper (or finger to keyboard), there are some issues that need to be addressed. A lot of writers out there think writing YA fiction is easy. It's not. Some mistakes you might make will condemn your book to languish on the slush pile forever. So before we even talk about the nitty-gritty of how to shape your book—character, plot, setting, point of view—we need to talk about the five key elements that can make or break you as a YA writer.

THE HOLDEN CAULFIELD RULE—DON'T BE A PHONY!

Imagine traveling to a planet where your survival depends on hiding out among the inhabitants, where being recognized as a phony would mean instant annihilation. In that situation, you'd want to study the locals until you knew just how to look and sound and respond like them. It is the same in YA fiction. In this case, sudden death occurs when the reader, stumbling upon a false image, loses interest. The book closes with the splintering sound of a fatal bullet.

It's no exaggeration.

Holden Caulfield, the protagonist of J. D. Salinger's *Catcher in the Rye*, was always railing against the phoniness of other people, particularly adults. The enduring popularity of *Catcher in the Rye* demonstrates that teens today are the same way—they despise fakes.

> **YA FICTION RULE #1:** THE LIFE OF THE STORY DEPENDS ON THE WRITER'S ABILITY TO CONVINCE READERS THAT THE PROTAGONIST IS ONE OF THEM.

The key to writing a successful YA novel means knowing kids well enough to channel their voices, thoughts, and emotions. ("Kids" is used as an operative word here. The official YA audience encompasses twelve- to eighteen-year-olds, but it is expanding as children's book publishers work to attract readers as young as ten and eleven, and adult publishers reach to capitalize on the growing market.) While some of your readers may be a little younger than the twelve-to-eighteen target—children aged ten to twelve tend to read above their age—and some may be a little older, keep in mind that you have to convince all segments of your audience that you know what it feels like to be a young person today. If you can't convince your audience that you know how they feel about the world today and express yourself the same way, you will never reach them.

AVOID THE PREACH 'N' TEACH

Whether YA readers attend elementary or secondary school isn't an issue when it comes to the importance of YA Fiction Rule #2.

> **YA FICTION RULE #2:** DON'T BE CONDESCENDING TO YOUR READERS.

Young people won't abide stories that suggest that their turmoil or idealism will pass when they "grow up." Brent Hartinger, author of *Geography Club*, says, "I'm a big believer that kids are smarter than we think they are....I think kids can handle complexity and nuances, and the advantage to writing that way is that the book appeals to both teenagers and adults."

Many adults read fiction as an escape—teens are no different. Imagine spending a long day in school, learning boring lessons 'cause you're supposed to, having everyone from parents to teachers to employers telling you what to do, how to think, what to wear, then picking up a novel—and having someone else trying to shove another lesson down your throat! I can't imagine a bigger letdown.

Don't deal with young people by trying to push them in one direction or another. Deal with them where they're at now.

SOAK IT UP!

A word of caution: don't emulate your favorite authors, but learn from them. You'll want to create work that is truly your own. In the resource guide at the back of this book, along with details such as schools that offer writing degrees with a YA focus, you'll find listings for websites that recommend great YA fiction.

> YA FICTION RULE #3: READ, READ, READ TODAY'S YA FICTION.

The benefits to reading what's already on the market are phenomenal. It will familiarize you with what's selling, how kids today talk, what they wear, what issues concern them, and so on. If you don't have easy access to a teen, reading books meant for teens is probably the next best thing to having a teen personally tell you what he or she would like to read.

IDEALS FIRST, MEALS LATER

Writing a successful book that aims to attract the widest possible audience should be every writer's goal, shouldn't it? The answer is yes and no. It helps to have a general audience age in mind, but you don't want to be consumed with thoughts about how and whether you'll sell your work.

> # YA FICTION RULE #4: SILENCE YOUR WORRIES ABOUT COMMERCIAL CONSIDERATIONS.

This allows you to concentrate on your primary objective, which is to tell your story. If a nagging inner voice surfaces or someone discourages you, rather than pulling on earphones and listening to music as a teenager might, transform the voices through the power of your imagination into "white noise." This is the all-frequency sound emitted from machines that imparts a feeling of privacy, calming you and allowing you to focus on that world you're creating. Keep your artistic integrity—your ideals—ahead of how commercially successful—your meals—you want your book to be. If you focus on writing the best possible book, commercial success will follow later.

As your manuscript develops while you work through the guidelines provided in the ensuing chapters, your audience will become as clear to you as if you were speaking on a stage and looking into an auditorium full of people. If you subsequently work with an agent, the two of you can determine whether the manuscript should be pitched to editors specializing in YA, adult fiction, or both. But the fate of your manuscript will still be up in the air. Editors, who are invested with the power to buy or decline a manuscript, will ultimately determine to whom the book will be marketed.

The significant rise in the success of YA novels has opened the way for a multiplicity of categories, and just to give you an idea, I've listed some alphabetically: adventure, chick lit, comical, fantasy, fantasy epics, futuristic, gay-themed, historical, multicultural, mystery, religious, romantic, science fiction, sports, and urban. If your story idea doesn't fit into any of these categories, you may have to invent one. Consider it an opportunity.

THE UNDISCOVERED COUNTRY

From this point on, let your creative spirit be guided by YA Rule #5.

> YA RULE #5: IN YOUR NEW WORLD OF YA FICTION, ERECT NO CONCRETE BARRIERS, WIRE FENCES, OR ONE-WAY SIGNS. INSTEAD, FORGE NEW PATHS.

The YA field welcomes innovators. Encapsulating the newness of the time, YA novels are being published in nontraditional formats. Three YA authors banded together to compose a novel. Another entry is an interactive book with websites that combines reading with the world of Internet gaming. What will your contribution be? Think fresh.

Remember that young people are trendsetters—they're always looking to differentiate themselves from others. It's how teens forge their own identities. Don't be afraid to push the boat out as well. Coming up with a fresh idea will set you apart from the pack and might be the thing that sparks an editor's interest in your work.

Okay, consider yourself warned. Now that you know what not to do, it's time to learn how to craft the next YA bestseller. Step by step, this book will walk you through the mechanics of what makes a great YA novel.

Chapter 2 is about generating an idea, your story. It will talk about different ways to uncover stories that YA readers will want to read about. It will also help you discover new possibilities for stories within yourself that you may not have known you had.

Chapter 3 will discuss characters—the heart of any manuscript. How to breathe life into interesting characters your reader will connect with is the main lesson of this chapter, but we'll also discuss how to find the best characters for the story you want to tell.

Chapter 4 is all about plot, story, and how to tell the difference. Plot is like a machine that propels your manuscript forward, while story is the overall impression you want the plot to create in the reader's mind.

Chapter 5 is about how to put together a believable plot. It's all about action—establishing the main conflict of your manuscript and putting it in motion. Of special concern will be integrating the events of the manuscript with the characters' personalities, making sure that the characters react to events in believable ways.

Chapter 6 is about setting and timeline. Setting is the background of your story—the when and where. This chapter is about understanding the atmosphere of your story and effectively manipulating the details of that atmosphere to influence your manuscript's tone.

Chapter 7 is about point of view—the perspective from which you tell your story. Point of view can be an extremely effective tool for connecting with character and clarifying or confusing the reader about events—provided you use it correctly.

Chapter 8 is about the meat of your manuscript—dialogue. Dialogue provides an opportunity for your characters to interact and opens up another way to build your characters.

Chapter 9 is about the theme of your manuscript. Theme is the overall impression you want your readers to take away. It's a subtle but effective way for the author to express himself through the story.

Chapter 10 is about wrapping it all up, bringing your plot to a successful resolution. Endings can be very tricky, so there will be detailed discussion about what sorts of conclusions to avoid.

Chapter 11 is about how to find constructive feedback and incorporate it into your revisions. All authors need to edit and revise their manuscript, and this chapter will explain why the editing process is so necessary.

Chapter 12 is about getting published—what agents and editors do and how to get your work into their hands. This is the business chapter—the one that details exactly how the publishing industry works.

Chapter 13 is about YA nonfiction and the emerging genre of New Adult. The YA market is constantly in flux, and this chapter will expose you to two recent developments in the market.

I hope all of these tools will be helpful to you as you begin the process of writing the next YA bestseller. Let's begin exploring that magical new world.

CHAPTER 2

ACCEPTING THE GIFT OF STORY

Some people think that stories can be found, but they cannot—the universe gives them to us. Once your ear is attuned, and if you keep an open mind, story ideas will rush to you. Accepting the gift of story can be as much of an adventure for the writer as it is for the reader. How can we discover the story that is in us? In this chapter I encourage you to try your hand at an unusual exercise to jog the creative process to find your own story idea.

EXERCISE: HISTORICAL IDEA

I challenged Leah, a would-be writer, to try this exercise for coming up with an idea for a historical novel. She said she wasn't interested in writing a historical novel (and you may not be either!), but I asked her to bear with me for the moment. I asked her to be prepared to start writing as she allowed her mind to travel back to another point in time that she'd either read about, heard of from others, or lived through—and to create a story line that could enhance the sense of feeling different. I'm asking you to do the same by opening a journal or Word document on your computer so that you'll be prepared to write. There are also a few blank lines provided here if you wish to take notes.

You know this is a dream, but there's no way to pull out of it. Besides, waking is the last thing you need. You're standing in your old bedroom where you spent much of your adolescence. There's a chill in the air, but you aren't cold. The floor creaks beneath your feet, but you're not intimidated. The curtains have grown threadbare, the carpet needs shampooing, but you're paying more attention to some old memories that are refracted in a streak of sunlight beaming through the open window. Yeah, there you were, a teenager in all your glory. But this is not the time to get distracted. You're here on a mission.

Where would you have hidden that diary? Many a night you poured your heart onto those pages. (So what if you never kept a diary; this is a dream, remember?)

Frustrated as you are at your lack of success at finding the diary, you can't help but be impressed with your new capabilities. All you have to do is think about searching way in the back of that high shelf, and the closet door flies open. Everything in the room seems to act in accordance with your intentions.

There's no need to look for a stepladder—you're tall enough to see the back of the shelf. The search continues as one by one dresser drawers open, their contents turned as if by a gentle unseen hand. Still, you wonder whether you should give up. This search seems to be futile.

And then you spot the diary lying right in the middle of your old bed. The search was completely unnecessary. Your diary was right where you needed it all along.

Excited about reading the contents, you turn through the pages, and somehow, you are not surprised to see that the day-to-day details of your teenage life have faded with time. The faint ink marks are indecipherable. Maybe in the past, a discovery such as this might have caused you to despair, but your mastery over this room and over your adolescence has convinced you that you already have everything you need to select the perfect topic for your young adult novel. The emotions you experienced as a teen are yours forever. They are also universal and capable of transcending time.

Nothing is lost or wasted on the pages of your adolescence. There are young people waiting to be brought to life. They are poised to act, feel, speak, and grow.

- ANATOMY LESSONS -

There's certainly no formula for writing a great opening chapter, but success or failure hinges on how well the writer pulls off the start of the work. If you don't grab your readers from the beginning, they'll just close the book. You may want to pull favorite YA novels off the shelf and reread opening chapters to see what made them work. For now, let's take a look at what prizewinning author Walter Mosley did in the opening pages of 47 to leave readers hungry for more. Let me count the ways in which he succeeds: (1) Mosley grounds us in a sense of place and time, revealing that the fourteen-year-old protagonist, known as number 47, is a slave living on a plantation. (2) He encourages empathy for this young man by tapping into universal fears of abandonment. 47's mother died when he was so young he could no longer remember her face, and he explains that only one adult on the plantation has shown him love and affection. (3) We are enticed with the mystery of who 47's father might be. (4) And 47 is placed in the eye of a dangerous emotional storm. His longing for the plantation owner's beautiful daughter could lead to his being killed in the most brutal fashion. Mosley's winning combination tugs at our hearts and compels us to keep turning the pages to discover what's going to happen to an adolescent who has so little in life that his name is only a number.

In this room of your mind, where you are master of your own kingdom, record succinctly a memory of feeling different from other teens.

_____

_____

_____

Now take that feeling of being different and use it as the basis for an idea for a historical novel.

....

....

....

It wasn't long before Leah wrote:

> It's the 1960s and a teenage girl is being raised by hippie parents in a rural commune. Alerted by a hostile neighbor, an official from the town's child protective service shows up. Finding that the girl is completely ignorant of basic facts, he insists that she enroll at the local public high school. On her first day of classes, she becomes the center of attention. Her suburban classmates want to know how to look like a sixties love child, the way she does, but they treat her as if she just stepped off the moon.

Leah, surprised and impressed with herself, remarked that she'd never thought of that idea before, and she liked it.

What about you? What idea did you come up with? Don't miss out on this opportunity to flex your creative muscles and dig up your emotional experiences of the past.

After you've come up with an idea for your own historical novel, you're ready for the next exercise.

EXERCISE: EXPLORING EMOTIONS

Write down the predominant emotions of your adolescence that caused strife in your life. Maybe you despised a sibling, felt ashamed of your family, or were terrified of a parent or other adult. Leah wrote that she felt (1) "shame about looking different from the other kids in my neighborhood," (2) "heartsick about a boy I loved," (3) "jealous because he loved my best friend," and (4) "sneaky, because I couldn't let my parents know what I was hiding."

Think back to what might have led you to write passionately in that imagined diary. I'm not asking for a specific incident here, but an emotion. You can record it below.

After you've recorded your predominant emotions, choose one or more that still resonates with you. When Leah said that sneaking around and not being able to reveal her true self was a major theme in her adolescence, I told her she was on the verge of coming up with another story idea. The same goes for you. What story line can you connect to that powerful emotion from the past?

STORY GIFTS

When she did the previous exercise, Leah wrote: "A teenage boy is terrified of telling his parents that he's gay. When he finally blurts it out, they're not only accommodating, but they go overboard trying to welcome his new identity."

Leah looked up wide-eyed from the page. These events had not happened to anyone she knew. She said, "I don't know where that story idea came from."

I did. I call these kinds of story ideas gifts from the universe. Now that you're opening your heart to them, they will begin to come at you at a fast clip. When writing YA fiction, you can use the emotions you experienced in the past to create an authentic story idea for whatever genre fits your writing style and interests. YA author Scott Westerfeld explored the desire that so many teens feel to look "prettier" to create his bestselling *Uglies*. He created a world of the future where citizens are brainwashed into believing they are so ugly they need to be surgically transformed. It's an idea that worked for him. *Uglies* was the first entry in a bestselling sci-fi trilogy that included *Pretties* and *Specials*.

Just as when you go to the gym and use machines that work muscles for various parts of your body, coming up with ideas for all types of genres will keep you at your creative best.

EXERCISE: REBELLION

One last part of this exercise of using emotions to empower story ideas involves adolescent rebellion. Young people often feel compelled to separate emotionally from their parents, so it's not surprising that they fight restraints by rebelling in one way or another. Think of an incident during adolescence when you were forced to do something, wear something, learn something, meet someone, or go somewhere against your wishes. Picture the event, and most important, remember how you felt. You'll want to record your emotions below.

....

....

....

Now go with those emotions, riding them like a wave. Come up with a story idea that arouses that emotion and explores a subculture.

....

....

....

Leah wrote:

After news of her uncle's death, a Japanese American girl is forced to relocate to Japan. Her father must take over his oldest brother's role of Shinto priest, while she must learn all the traditions and customs of her new country. She'd always complained about the kids at her American school, but once she's in Japan, she finds herself idealizing the life she left behind.

What cultural story is waiting to be told by you? Marjane Satrapi used a graphic format with simple and yet moving black-and-white illustrations in *Persepolis* to provide a glimpse of life in Iran through the eyes of a rebellious adolescent who loves Nikes and Iron Maiden. Her autobiographical book became the subject for a popular film of the same title.

"!!" - ADVICE FROM PUBLISHERS ROW -

Julia Richardson, editorial director at Houghton Mifflin Harcourt and editor of the bestselling *Crank* by Ellen Hopkins:

"Start a novel in a place that allows you to weave in a little background. Hold off on introducing readers to the big problem the protagonist is going to encounter. I want to know what that character's world is like when it's normal so that we can see the catalyst for change.

"But with that said, you shouldn't necessarily open your story at the beginning of the character's day. I worked with a group at a writers conference, and everybody began with the kid waking up and then something horrible happened. Ask yourself, what is life like for this character? And work hard on the voice. Whether speaking or thinking, the voice should sound raw and immediate and youthful in a lifelike way. That requires you to be familiar with kids and understand what's going on in their lives today. As a kid I loved to read about experiences that I never wanted to experience in real life. Whenever

ACCEPTING THE GIFT OF STORY

I did go through something difficult, I would think about how one of my favorite characters got through it. My parents separated when I was fourteen, and as hard as it was for me, I felt I'd already survived it, because I'd read Judy Blume's *It's Not the End of the World* [Yearling, 1972]. It was nice knowing that someone I trusted had been through it before."

Daniel Ehrenhaft, editorial director at Soho Teen:

"I feel that you should write something that is meaningful to you. The quicker you can get to the meat of the story, sure, that's helpful. But reducing everything because you have to sell it internally instead of thinking about characters or a story you want to tell is going about it backwards."

OTHER WAYS TO GENERATE IDEAS

The rule for writing used to be to write only what you know. That's no longer the case. It's a definite advantage to have lived in the country where your story is set, but don't let foreigner status hold you back. A guidebook and the Internet can bring a country and its people up close.

Sometimes, publishers will conceptualize and/or generate their own ideas inside the publishing house and then reach out to agents and/or authors directly to find a writer. When this occurs, publishers call it an IP project. IP (intellectual property) is legalese for an idea. Daniel Ehrenhaft explains: "The idea can be a paragraph or it can be five pages, but the publisher controls all the rights and subrights. For example, we conceived of an idea about dancer with a psychic gift. Then the author took the idea and turned it into *Dancer, Daughter, Traitor, Spy*—something way better than we could have ever imagined." Intellectual property collaborations can help you explore ideas you may have never considered on your own, but because the project was generated in-house, it organically has the support of the entire team. When working on an IP project, be sure that you get an agent to work with you on sharing as many rights as possible with the publisher.

Here are some other suggestions for coming up with story ideas:

- **Keep up with the news:** Trends can lead the way to a plot. What are statistics telling us about youth culture? Is there a story there? But don't get stuck thinking the only news stories that can offer up ideas have to focus on young people. Flip news articles around and think of them from an adolescent's perspective. Let's say you're reading about homeowners losing their houses during a national real estate crisis. Consider the shame that's involved, which might lead you to a story about a teen whose house goes into foreclosure. After the rug is pulled out from beneath her, she begins living a lie about her family's circumstances.

  Milk interesting television news features to find out whether they offer story potential. An article about a Hassidic Jewish principal running a tough inner-city school might offer a germ of an idea. Think of that same story from the point of view of one of his students—and then go with the emotions. A young person enrolled in his school might be feeling hopelessness, despair, anger, or perhaps the desire to flee. How might this new principal shake up this character's life?

- **Listen to conversations:** Think of yourself as having roving ears, always on the hunt for snippets of conversations. Spend time in a Starbucks located near a high school and keep your ears open. You might overhear someone saying, for instance, that she has a crush on the father of the child she babysits. Can you do anything with that? There's always a possibility.

- **Go on Facebook:** Young people can't seem to get enough of baring their souls online. Read what they're saying on this or other social networking sites.
- **Join organizations that cater to young people:** If you don't have any young people in your life, volunteer to work for a youth program.
- **Watch shows featuring adolescents:** You might enjoy watching a singing competition that includes a beautiful young vocalist right on the cusp of stardom. But since you're always wearing your writer's cap, your imagination is helping you come up with the story of an adolescent whose world seems perfect until she realizes that her life is trapped in a TV reality show, and that any decisions she makes will always be decided by her voting audience.

By now you've got the picture. Consider your mind a giant search machine, shifting through events that occur around you. From here on, consider every situation as a potential ingredient for a story.

Remember, teens live in the same world you do. TV, war, blogging, the economy, music, the Internet—these things affect their lives just as much as they do yours. One way of connecting with your audience, as well as coming up with your material for your next bestseller, is to see the world through their eyes. In the next chapter you'll learn to create characters, which are the embodiments of your youthful emotions.

- AUTHOR WORKING -

Ellen Hopkins, author of *Crank* and several other fast-paced bestsellers that feature risk-taking adolescents:

"Teens tell me that when they're reading my books, they feel as if their lives aren't so bad. I don't pretend that terrible things don't happen to kids, because they do. My next book [*Identical*, Simon & Schuster, 2008] is about incest. I got the idea from talking to two strong, successful friends who went through that. I want readers to know that although they will always feel haunted by ghosts, they can move on and have successful lives. In all my books I try to show not just what's happening to the main characters, but to the people around them. Once I get an idea, I research it and then conduct as many personal interviews as I can. My next book will be on teen prostitutes, so I contacted people at rescue organizations and talked to them about how they help, and then I talked to the teens. The average age for a teen prostitute is twelve. It's important for writers to follow a story idea to where it leads them. This prostitution book started out as one that I intended to write on teen gambling. But when one of the characters turned out to be a prostitute who was trying to support a gambling addiction, I found that the story's energy had shifted in that direction."

CHAPTER 3

MEETING YOUR CHARACTERS

The people who populate your narrative and propel your plot forward are your characters. Without them there's really no fiction. A story exists because something happens to someone that forces him or her to change and grow. The protagonist is the main character around whom most of the action is centered. The distinctiveness of your characters will, to a large extent, determine the success of your novel. This chapter will help you create one or more YA protagonists and secondary characters.

It's easy enough to base your main character on someone you have heard about from friends and acquaintances or who you have learned of from the media. Or you can adapt characters directly from your life. You may know fascinating people who would fit perfectly into a work of fiction. And while you can certainly integrate disguised versions of real-life people into your story, your goal should be to create a new and improved version of the real thing.

After reading this chapter, you may find that characters start walking into your imagination uninvited. You might find yourself rushing from the shower or waking at night to scribble details into a notebook that you keep nearby for moments such as these, and you'll hardly be able to write quickly enough to transcribe the details.

As you begin this process, remind yourself that there are no mistakes in character development. Be prepared to begin with a main character who evolves eventually into someone completely different from the model with which you began. After all, that's why this process is called character "development." The individual you imagine begins with just a grain of an idea, and by the time you finish, it's as if you've raised a whole real person out of nothing. Let your characters take you places you hadn't expected to go—that's often the sign of an interesting, three-dimensional character others will want to read about. So let's get started.

FIRST STEPS

You've already come up with an idea for a story, and now you can continue by developing characters who fit credibly into your plotline. It's a given that your protagonist must be twelve to eighteen years old, in keeping with the interests of YA readers. The specific age will be determined by your story circumstances and the need to maintain credibility.

To give your imagination a nudge, pretend you're a judge for a reality television show writing an advertisement seeking contestants. This will force you to make some decisions, because the wording for the ad you publish to attract contestants should be determined by your expectations for these people and the broad circumstances and situations they will face.

So how about your protagonist? What does she have to pull off? Think of various scenes that fit within your scenario. Depending upon the plot, a writer might want a main character who can do one or more of the following: drive a car, lead a gang, speak compellingly about love to someone of the opposite sex, or scamper up a mountain. After you have imagined your character in various scenes that fit within your story, come up with an age and a personality description.

I've written a rudimentary story to use as an illustration that can help you learn how to do this. Let's say I'm writing a YA novel about a young man who is worried about his mother's well-being and is suspicious of his stepfather's motives. In order for my protagonist to credibly take on his stepfather and pose some kind of threat, intellectually or physically, this young man would have to be at least fifteen. In addition, I wouldn't want him to be too young to be able to live on his own. I also would want him to be likable, to draw a contrast between the stepfather and son. Now, what kind of situation would make a boy suspicious of his stepfather's motives? Perhaps the mother is emotionally vulnerable but has a considerable amount of money—in that case I'll need a teen who is a little uncomfortable with living in an upscale neighborhood, but dresses well because his family can afford it. As the mother has been fragile for most of my character's life, he's good at talking to adults but is fed up with always having to parent his mother. To that end, my ad reads:

Wanted

> Handsome sixteen-year-old male, unaware of his good looks and capable of looking wealthy. He must have excellent manners and a good command of English. He'll also have to act embarrassed by his family's wealth and its trappings. The character is sweet but a brooder, and loves his mom but is desperate to put distance between him and her. An only child, this character feels he's alone in this world, despite his mother's love, because she is too distracted to offer him protection.

Now write your own want ad. Keep in mind that my ad touched upon a classic and not-easily-exhausted theme for young adult stories: kids with parents who are not readily available to rush in and help. The very idea touches upon a young person's greatest fears.

Now let's consider what kind of people you should audition for your protagonist.

- Does this character have a distinctive way of speaking?
- Any particular habits, favorite sports, or activities?
- Any nervous tics or passions?
- What sort of music does he/she like? Who are his/her favorite bands?
- What are his/her ambitions in life?
- What would this character's friends say about him/her?
- Whom, in this character's life, are they close to?
- What does this character want most? What does he/she fear most?
- Is he/she shy or bold, loquacious or sullen?
- Successful in school or an academic disappointment? Any favorite subjects in school?
- What do his/her teachers think of him/her?
- Popular with peers or an outcast?
- Who are this character's mentors? Whom does he/she look up to?
- What irritates or embarrasses this character?

Once you've had a chance to think through the answers to some of these questions, you'll want to weave your answers into a want ad:

My Want Ad

....

....

....

CHOOSING YOUR CHARACTERS

Okay, you posted an imaginary want ad and look at what you got for your trouble. There's a never-ending line of imaginary characters waiting just outside your consciousness, prepared to audition for the role. Remember to think of yourself as a reality show judge. You're looking for something specific, and you want to know how each character matches up with what you're looking for. You can begin interviewing one applicant after another. Think of the things you need to know about them. What do they need to do or say to convince you to write about them? What sort of performance do they give? Be skeptical—force them to impress you. Think about how they measure up in comparison with the other candidates.

As you conduct interviews, be sure to keep careful notes by recording the details of the most promising characters. What are their names? Who would be the best fit for your story? What do they look like? Observe them from head to toe. As patterns emerge, describe physical details, such as weight, height, hair color and style, and the kind of clothes each character wears.

Out of all the people I interviewed who fit my job description, I chose sixteen-year-old Taylor Bradford of San Diego. He shows up in the middle of my scene wearing a 10.Deep urban street-wear hoodie and khaki shorts, his feet clad in Vans, and his long brown hair brushing his slender shoulders. With a matter-of-fact look on his face, my potential hero rolls into the scene on a skateboard, speeding along the driveway of his family's turn-of-century, Spanish-style mansion. Bounding up the steps, Taylor pushes open the unlocked door, and with a sudden burst of fury, he slams it shut.

And let's stop here. Now I know some basics about my character and what he looks like. But who is Taylor? Why should our reader care about him? Most important, what could compel the reader to keep turning the pages to learn his story? Those are important questions. What your main character wears, how your character looks, and what he says or does are important, but he won't become a fully fleshed character until you populate his universe. Let's look at how to do this.

"!!"

- ADVICE FROM PUBLISHERS ROW -

Nancy Mercado, editorial director of Scholastic Press:

"To my mind, a common mistake is thinking that every teen is a sullen, cantankerous misanthrope and therefore his character is one-dimensional."

Cecile Goyette, executive editor at Blue Apple Books:

"I feel that teens are unfortunately too often pandered to with thin stereotypes of whiny-bored-sullen characters. Characters that are interesting and who search and struggle and have some level of sincerity (however well-guarded, indefensible, or twisted!) offer rich opportunities for emotional connections."

Jennifer Hunt, former editorial director at Little Brown Children's Books:

"When I read *Story of a Girl* by Sara Zarr for the first time, I fell in love with the voice. Sara Zarr definitely has the teenage voice when it comes to respecting emotions. Sometimes in order to find that voice, you have to try it several times before you get it right. Authors need to truly examine the issues that the character is facing from 360 degrees. When the character has an original voice and it's coupled with a great plotline, that's what makes a book truly distinctive."

Wendy Lamb, publisher of Wendy Lamb Books:

"Remember that most adolescents naturally live at a very high emotional pitch. Your characters should reflect that intensity—but they should not feel strident or forced."

Kat Brzozowski, associate editor at Thomas Dunne Books/St. Martin's Press:

"When I start reading a manuscript, I look for a strong

voice carried across all genres. And while edgy may be popular, an author should never write towards a trend because it often comes off forced or inauthentic. It's more important to write the story you're meant to write, whether that's edgy or not."

ADDING CHARACTER EMOTION AND DEPTH

Once you've conducted a number of fantasy interviews and have come up with a working prototype, now's the time to give your protagonist a sense of character. When I refer to character in this instance, I'm talking about moral substance, strength of will, integrity or lack thereof. Your main character should be someone the reader can trust to behave in a consistent fashion. That doesn't mean this person is always virtuous; that would make for dull reading. I mean that the character's behaviors remain consistent with who we know him to be over time. Of course a character's moral development can be weighted by circumstances that are laid bare to the reader.

Because we are writing about humans (or at least animals or aliens with human emotions and dreams), a character can't be brought to life without interaction with others. As social animals, we are largely defined by our relationships. That's especially the case for young adults, for whom peer relationships often take precedence over familial ties. This holds true for those who feel alienated as well as for those who are slavishly attached to the crowd. Adolescents define themselves through interaction with their peers.

For illustrative purposes, let's return to the main character I'm developing. By now readers might be wondering about Taylor: Is this guy a spoiled brat, or what? Where did his family get all that dough? And what the heck is he so angry about anyway?

The general rule is to allow your character's actions to speak louder than your explanations. If you gain your reader's trust, he or she will wait for all to be revealed in due time.

Upon entering the house, Taylor hears his mom calling, but he rushes from the sound of her voice, not pausing until he's in his room. Leaning against the closed bedroom door, he wishes he could stop his mom from walking in and telling him what he doesn't want to hear. But she's already in the hallway, and then knocking hesitantly, to which he grumbles something akin to "Come in."

> Taylor turns on his computer and taps a few keys, any excuse to avoid making eye contact. He doesn't have to look up to see her. He already knows that she's young for a mother, too young to have lost a husband and to have raised a son alone. The two of them learned to depend on each other, and they were close, at least they had been close until she married Frank...that clown.
>
> "So..." she says, casting her gaze around the room. He can see her by sneaking shy looks from under his heavy lashes. As long as he can remember, she has been determined to befriend instead of parent him. She's biting her lip now, as if holding back complaints about the clothes-strewn floor and junked-up room.
>
> And his mom is stalling, he notices, which means the news she's about to deliver has got to be the absolute worst, and it is.
>
> "Frank did accept the job, Taylor. We're moving to Brazil."

Now do you feel more sympathy for Taylor than before? This is key in creating a good character. You want your reader to feel sympathy, understand, and care for your protagonist as he becomes more finely nuanced. And the best way to get these attributes across is through your main character's interactions with other characters. Taylor, for instance, grown weary of his mother's obliviousness and his stepfather's lack of integrity, may throw all caution to the wind and commit an act that he later regrets, but this would be fully understandable given his circumstances.

As you do reveal the heart of your protagonist, make sure his behavior seems in keeping with his character. For instance, Taylor may make it a point to never look his mother in the eyes. I don't think that's because he's a shady, unpredictable louse or even because he sees himself in her reflection—he's not that introspective. I think it's because he's frightened by her weakness. She's making decisions that will change the course of their lives, and he needs to feel assured that there's a grown-up in the house. No wonder he's so angry.

Keep in mind that what separates the YA protagonist from any other is that his or her emotional reaction almost always involves peers, and that will offer clues about his character. Ask yourself how your main character will react inwardly and outwardly to the dilemmas you pose. For instance, Taylor may love his mother and feel fiercely protective of her, but his response to moving to another country will certainly involve a longing to commune with other young people. He's terrified of flying without a safety net. Will that girl he likes at school forget him? Will there be new kids he can identify with in Brazil? And most important, will they accept him? These are questions of paramount importance in a YA novel.

Now that his mother has decided to move to Brazil, Taylor is forced to choose between the familiar and the exotic. Should he put up a fight and refuse to go? Will he accuse her of destroying his life? And is he a fighter?

I hate to be the first to inform you, but you won't get to decide one way or another. You're developing a flesh-and-blood teenager with a heart that beats. He's not going to let anyone tell him anything. He gets to decide what he wants to do. And it will be easier for you to listen for how your main character wants to respond if you start compiling his history, which is often called a backstory.

The backstory includes details that you may or may not weave into the plot. You write a backstory because this is your opportunity to get to know your protagonist. It's as if you have a weekend away together and you get a chance to really talk; only you're remaining quiet and allowing him to do all the sharing.

To start creating your protagonist's backstory, list everything that comes to mind about him that you want to flesh out. Your list should grow eventually into several pages and should start out looking something along these lines, as mine would with Taylor:

1. He pretends he doesn't care squat about his appearance but hates seeing himself in a photo or mirror. He brushes his teeth and combs his hair in the bathroom with the lights turned out.

2. He has tucked beneath his box springs a crumpled photo of himself at the age of three sitting on his dad's shoulders. When he's distressed, he talks to the photo.

3. He's about to go into his senior year, and he knows if he puts up a big enough fight, his mom would let him stay in the States with his aunt.

4. Taylor won't ask to say behind, because he's afraid his mom would agree, and he just can't let her go that far away with Frank on her own.

5. There's something waiflike, naïve, undeveloped about his mother.

6. Taylor goes through Frank's paperwork. His mother's new husband is a complete mystery to him, and he can't understand why his mom was crazy enough to marry that clown. Frank claimed he was selling his house and business when he moved to join them in San Diego, but the guy never gets any mail or anything that would suggest he has closed down a business or a home.

7. Taylor is growing a beard, but when his mother notices over breakfast and rubs his chin, he blows up.

8. While in Brazil, Taylor falls in love. The young lovers can't speak the same language, but they communicate nevertheless.
9. His mom is hiding a secret from Taylor: she's pregnant with Frank's child.
10. In Brazil, Taylor practices some native traditions that annoy Frank.

In the coming days, continue adding to your backstory as you get ideas from studying other people, reading, and watching TV and other forms of entertainment. Soon enough some items on your list will seem contradictory or out of tune, in which case you should drop them or make adjustments. Remember, this is not a list of ideas that advance the plot. As a fly on the wall you get to see this character up close, and through your observations come to know more about him than he even knows himself.

- ANATOMY LESSONS -

James Patterson is the bestselling author of adult thrillers who also writes the YA bestselling Maximum Ride series. The main character of that series, Max, is the leader of five other flying kids who were engineered in a laboratory. Max can make fast work of ruthless predators and fly at two hundred miles per hour, but Patterson grounds this exotic character in reality. Max longs for what most teenage girls take for granted, like dating a cute guy and overeating at Thanksgiving. Since Max has had to learn to be wary of people, when she does let her guard down and gets hurt, readers feel her loss deeply. In *Maximum Ride: School's Out Forever*, Max must leave behind one of her fellow flock members after reuniting him with his parents.

Looking around the room, she observes that everyone else is on the verge of tears. Although brokenhearted herself, Max maintains her sarcastic tough-girl veneer, thinking, "I hate stuff like this, where everyone's overwhelmed and weeping with joy and emotions are splashing all over the place. Ugh." Because readers are tied into Max, we cry for her, even though she can't afford to. Patterson's success in the YA field is a reminder that readers don't keep returning to a series just because of the plots, but also because they're eager to reunite with literary friends.

SECONDARY CHARACTERS

You can create a second protagonist, should your story call for one, by following your main character's lead. You don't have to go back to the interviewing technique, unless you want to, because if a second protagonist is required, you will find that this person is so integral to the developing story that executing the plot would seem impossible without him.

As your protagonist is brought to life, you will also be introduced to the secondary characters who will populate his universe. You will want to keep the number of characters to a memorable eight or even fewer. There's nothing more annoying to readers than having to turn back to recall who's who. But don't worry about character counts as you start your novel.

After finishing a first draft, ask members of your writing group (if you have one) or someone else you respect to offer comments. If you're told that the characters are difficult to distinguish from one another, you may have some cutting to do. If that is the case, try playing around with merging two or more characters. For instance, Taylor has grown to depend upon his family's housekeeper and her husband, the chauffeur. But because the cast is becoming unwieldy, I might find it necessary to kill off one of my darlings and get rid of the chauffeur, giving the housekeeper more to do.

MOTIVATION

Finally, let me offer one last word about your main character's behavior. Take time to understand and communicate his motivation. Here's how I view motivation: if your protagonist is the embodiment of your story, his motivation is your literary lifeblood, the often unstated explanation for why this character is willing to go to such great lengths and endure difficult circumstances.

Make sure you imply in the plot why your character is motivated to follow a certain course of action. The motivation of the protagonist in my plot, for instance, hinges on Taylor's sense that his mother is too weak to survive Frank's evil nature. Still, Taylor is considering staying put until he overhears that his mother is expecting a child. Taylor is determined to keep the baby safe. Your motivation should be in keeping with the protagonist's character. The motivation that explains why Taylor is willing to move would not be credible were he not a very mature kid, with legitimate reasons for worrying about his stepfather's morality.

Taylor suspects that Frank is moving his mom away from familiar climes so that he can take her for everything she's worth. The cross-purposes of the two—Taylor, the protagonist, who's determined to save his mom and her unborn child, and the antagonist, Frank, who may in fact be planning to get his hands on his wife's wealth—intensifies the plot and makes it all the more intriguing.

Finally, when a protagonist resists an opposing force, you can write power-packed scenes. Consider, for instance, Taylor's last view of his childhood home.

The limo has pulled up, Taylor is insisting on carrying an oversized suitcase on his own, and as the three leave the house for what feels like the last time, Taylor stops to check the front door, which his mother usually leaves unlocked. But Frank steps forward, a muscular arm barring Taylor's way. "I already took care of it, kid," he sneers at Taylor. "You gotta let me be the man in the family."

Not likely, Taylor thinks, balling his hands into fists. His mother steps lightly toward the limo, her gait signaling her excitement about their new life.

Taylor checks his anger. This is not the time to fight, he tells himself, but soon, soon enough.

Whatever your story is, strong characters with their own motivation will make or break your novel. If it isn't clear why your characters react the way they do to their circumstances, your reader will lose interest and stop caring about them.

Vivid, engaging characters can act as a reader's best friend, alter ego, mentor, frenemy, or the family member they never had. When you bring a character to life, readers will follow him anywhere.

"!!" - ADVICE FROM PUBLISHERS ROW -

Evette Porter, publisher at EP Publishing:

"The novice writer will try to tell too many stories in a single novel. They try to throw everything in with the kitchen sink. At the core of any novel you need to have a clear and concise plot. A subplot is designed to enhance the main story line, and if it doesn't it's a distraction. In much the same way you would pitch a movie or television script, you should be able to articulate the core story line of your novel. If you can't tell what your story is about in a synopsis or outline, you won't be able to write a readable novel. However, subplots can be used to develop sequels and this technique is popular for those publishers like Harlequin. We look for series opportunities."

Daniel Ehrenhaft, editorial director at Soho Teen:

"My house almost never signs series. We typically sign a book with an option for a next book. We're the kind of publisher that does stand-alone mysteries maybe with one sequel. I'm always very excited to see what authors come up with next, as a fan of their work, and if for some reason one of our titles should make the bestseller list, then I'm open to exploring if we can turn it into a series."

CHAPTER 4

UNDERSTANDING PLOT

So what's your manuscript's story? And what's the plot? What's the difference anyway?

Many people don't know the difference between a novel's story and its plot. This chapter is designed to help you articulate your novel's story and to teach you how to construct a well-crafted plot. By learning the difference, you'll learn how to propel your manuscript forward and gain an understanding of the overall concept of your novel—its story.

PLOT VS. STORY

The most important point in this chapter is that plot is not story. The story of the novel is the full sequence of events in a work of fiction as the reader imagines them to have taken place, in the order in which they would have occurred in life.

Stories can be plot-driven or character-driven.

- **Plot-driven:** A plot-driven story is one in which a preconceived story line is the main thrust and the character's behavior is constantly being molded by the inevitable sequence of events that leads to the climax.
- **Character-driven:** A character-driven story is one in which the character is the main focus. Character-driven stories tend to be literary, and the story is a study of human behavior,

emotions, internal conflict, and personal weaknesses. The pivotal point of a character-driven story is when the protagonist understands his weakness and takes the first steps to overcome it.

Generally, novels for young adult readers are plot-driven and not character-driven, although the separation between the two types of story consists of a vast gray area where characteristics of both types may be found. Due to their lack of maturity, introspective ability, and experience, most young adult readers generally cannot understand and appreciate a character-driven story consisting of narration of human internal conflicts.

A plot is a chain of events where each event has a cause. Each event then becomes the cause of other events along the chain that leads to the climax of the story. Plot extends well beyond the boundaries of the story both into the past and the future. However, the author does not always explain every connection of the events to the lives of the characters. Often this insight is reserved for the reader, drawing him more deeply into the world of the story.

There are three kinds of plots:

- **Integrated:** An integrated plot is one where the story and the plot are tightly bound together and the cause-and-effect events of the plot drive the characters toward resolving the conflict at the climax. The vast majority of young adult plots are integrated.
- **Episodic:** An episodic plot is composed of loosely connected incidents, each one more or less self-contained. They are often connected by a central theme, location, conflict, or character. At times the distinction between an episodic novel and a collection of short stories with the same theme is not clear. Ray Bradbury's *Martian Chronicles* is an example of an episodic novel.
- **None:** Plotless stories are extremely rare in young adult

literature. An example of a plotless story would be Ernest Hemingway's *Big Two-Hearted River*, in which the meaning of the story is entirely symbolic. Stories like this are an illumination of life—the point seems to be "this is what life is about."

TYPES OF PLOTS

In the canon of literature all of the broad categories of conflicts have been in use since before the ancient Greeks. There are no new plots, only new ways to use them.

How many plots are there? That depends on how they are categorized. Pick a number from five to fifty, and a list of plots can be found for that number. Seven plots, which only slightly overlap one another, are generally mentioned by many writers.

- Man versus nature
- Man versus man
- Man versus the environment
- Man versus machine or technology
- Man versus the supernatural
- Man versus himself
- Man versus God or religion

Since there are no unique plots, the quality of a work of fiction rests on the author's ability to guide the trajectory of the plot and use it to build an original, interesting story. Most novels follow a familiar plot structure that forms the foundation for telling the story.

PLOT STRUCTURE

Many of the ideas about plot can be traced back to Aristotle in the guidelines he set out in his *Poetics*, written in 350 BC. Aristotle used the term *mythos* to denote plot and wrote that it is "the arrangement of incidents." From Aristotle, Freytag's pyramid was developed in 1863, which divided a story into five actions: exposition, complication, crisis, anticlimax, and resolution. Modern novels use a similar plot structure by adding two actions, creating a seven-step progression of action that flows through the novel. These are ground state, conflict/incitement, complications/rising action, crisis, climax, falling action, and denouement.

1. Ground State
As the story begins, the characters in their world are in a stable situation.

2. Conflict and Incitement
The stability of the characters' world is upset as a result of a conflict that confronts the protagonist. In modern young adult fiction this must happen immediately, with one or more conflicts arising or implied in the first few pages.

One of these conflicts faced by the protagonist is considered the incitement or the event that actually sets the chain of events of the plot in motion. Some authors, especially in mysteries, may deliberately set out false conflicts. In Alfred Hitchcock's movies these false conflicts often took the form of McGuffins—ideas or objects around which the plot revolves. While the characters may care deeply about what the McGuffin is, viewers typically care more about the characters and how they react to it. Although the McGuffin set the plot in motion, its exact nature—a government secret (*The 39 Steps*), a possible murder (*Rear Window*), $40,000 (*Psycho*)—was more or less interchangeable and unimportant.

3. Complications and Rising Action
Until the resolution of the story's central problem, the protagonist's situation should steadily get worse. A protagonist who finds many natural or unexplained obstacles in his path is "unlucky." On the other hand, a protagonist who is dealing with obstacles generated

by other characters is being "thwarted." The difficulties should increase primarily as a result of action by the protagonist, not just from outside forces. Every attempt at a solution should create a new and more tenacious problem as a result of that action. The objective is to create a steadily increasing suspenseful atmosphere in order to pull the reader into the story and to keep him reading to find what happens to the characters.

4. Crisis

In young adult stories this is the point of maximum tension and suspense just before the climax. Every event and plot twist has logically led to this point following the actions of the characters reacting to the cause of events. The final crisis is the result of bringing together all of the known information with some final crucial element that brings the entire story into focus in the mind of the reader.

At no time in the crisis scene should the author attempt to summarize the plot or give the reader hints as to the outcome. Trust the reader. If the story is clearly written with a strong, well-organized plot, he'll get it.

5. Climax

When a problem is resolved or an obstacle overcome, there is a climactic point of tension and drama in the story. The situation is such that the conflict must be resolved one way or the other when a character takes decisive action to end it. However, not all climactic points are created equal, and they should not have equal weight in the story. At the beginning of the story the plot should allow the protagonist small successes. As the story progresses, the challenges should increase in difficulty and the resulting climax should become more significant, leading up to the final central climax of the story. This is the high point of interest or suspense. The reader experiences the greatest emotional response to a character's problem at this point.

In retrospect the climax should not be a complete surprise. Immediately after the reader says, "Yeah, I got it," he should say, "Of course! I should've seen it." The story has been building to this one scene, and the reader should be familiar with all of the plot elements but would not have put them together in that particular form.

The final climax must be shown in a fully developed scene; none of the details of this final scene can be described out of the sight of the reader. At the climax circumstances change and the world of the protagonist becomes stable again.

6. Falling Action

Directly following the climax, the author should tie up all the loose ends of the story and briefly examine the consequences of the climax and changed world of the characters. If a problem or question has arisen, the author should deal with it before the end of the story. This can be as simple as a few lines describing the resolution or an acknowledgment that the problem isn't going to be solved within the space of this story. At the end of a story, a reader shouldn't be asking, "What about...?"

7. Denouement (Ending)

This is a French term meaning "unraveling." Most young adult authors prefer to leave most, if not all, of the meanings of the plot for the reader to figure out. That is, they will use indirection and suggestion rather than telling the reader right out. This gives the reader the opportunity to create his own interpretation of the story, which may be different from the author's. It also provides the opportunity to tempt the reader with further adventures of the same characters in the next book. There are a number of common endings for a plot.

- **Resolution:** This is the end of the conflict by the victory of one side or the other. One of the most common endings in young adult fiction, it does not always mean that the victory is entirely complete or satisfying to the characters. Resolutions with a small but noticeable element of failure, sacrifice, or loss add emotional depth and force the reader into a variety of interpretations of the ending and how the protagonist handles failure.
- **Revelation:** This is the exposure of something previously hidden in the plot. An example of a revelation ending is the short story "The Lottery" by Shirley Jackson. The lottery process occupies the entire story, and only in the last few paragraphs does the reader understand the purpose of the lottery.
- **Decision:** This ending comes when the protagonist makes up his mind about the conflict. The decision should be important, difficult, and require that the character give something up to gain much more.
- **Explanation:** This ending provides the solution for a mystery or a puzzle-type plot to the reader. An explanation ending works when the mystery or puzzle is sufficiently hidden that the reader will not usually be able to figure it out.
- **Trick:** This is a surprise and may be a jarring departure from the expected ending. William Sydney Porter (O. Henry) wrote hundreds of stories with trick endings. Trick endings are sometimes used in young adult fiction, but the danger is that readers may think the ending is too simple and may be disappointed. A trick ending works when the protagonist must make a difficult decision and the author keeps the reader from knowing what the protagonist will do.

An author must write his ending on that fine line between a clichéd plot where everything falls into place and the reader saw it coming three chapters ago, and a plot that mimics life too closely and just ends in the middle of nowhere.

SUBPLOTS

The author may choose to tell several stories at the same time—stories within a story. Along with the major plot there may be one or more subplots about other characters or about the protagonist. Subplots are used to add layers of obstacles, mystery, and suspense to the story. A subplot can also add past information, usually something the main character wasn't previously aware of. There are two types of subplots.

- **Parallel:** In a parallel subplot the author moves from the main plot to a subplot, using each to dramatize the other, bring in details from another time or place that affect the main plot, or compare and contrast different issues.
- **Hinged:** A subplot that dramatically joins and becomes part of the main plot at some point is called a hinged plot.

Generally, although there are exceptions, a subplot should not be introduced at the beginning of a novel. Subplots should support the protagonist. His actions should be introduced first and the subplots after.

Subplots can add layers of complexity to your novel and help add color to your story and your characters. But be careful how you use them. Remember they're subplots—subservient to your main plot. Your main plot should always come first.

CHAPTER 5

BUILDING YOUR PLOT

Given knowledge of the structure of a plot, how does an author develop a plot upon which to build a story that will take a reader on a satisfying fictional journey?

GENERAL GUIDELINES

The following suggestions will give you some ideas on how typical YA plots unfold.

Start the Story Early

The action of the story should begin as close to the beginning of the novel as possible. Long expositions and backstory will quickly lose the interest of young adult readers. An author who adds a prologue to his novel is kidding himself if he thinks the reader won't recognize it for what it is: backstory. The characters should have a short period of stability, reach the incitement point, establish the conflict, and take off running toward the climax as soon as possible. Backstory and exposition should be added a little at a time as the story progresses at points where it is required to move the plot forward.

Let the Characters Influence the Plot

A character in a particular situation will react in a wide variety of ways based on his personality and the relationships he may have to other characters and the setting. If the entire plot is worked out in advance and the author simply peoples it with characters to carry out the action, the characters will seem stiff and unreal because they are being forced away from who they are and how they would naturally react.

Don't Have Too Much Plot

Characters do not have to have a crisis or deal with threats every few pages. Too many characters, story lines, subplots, and too much action will quickly lose younger readers. Breaks in the action are important for the characters to reflect on what has happened, consider the current situation, and plan their next move. This will help sustain the suspense and ramp up the anticipation of watching the character move into the next action scene. The author should focus on the protagonist and his reactions to advance the story.

Let Readers Wait

Be sure the reader has all the information he needs to understand the plot and the action, but not so much that he knows the resolution of the conflict before the climax is reached. Anticipation creates empathy with the characters and keeps the reader involved in the story to find out what happens.

Pace the Plot

Imagine the plot as a wave flowing through the story with distinct patterns of up-and-down motions. The character begins in calm water as he considers the situation. As tension builds, he is on the upward slope of the wave, and at the crest a climax occurs and he drops back down into calm water. Each climax crest becomes larger and larger until the final, highest crest at the story climax. The increasingly larger waves sustain the tension until the end.

Let the Characters Grow

This is a requirement for quality young adult fiction. In most YA novels the characters are young. Psychologically, physiologically, and emotionally, these characters are not adults and do not have adult maturity. Dealing with the conflict and the climax will add a layer of experience to their personalities that must be reflected in their behavior at the end of the novel. It's essential that the author make the young reader a part of the story so that he can live vicariously through the protagonist and have the same experiences. In the end, the question with young adult fiction is, What did the reader carry away from the story? How is he different?

You've had a chance to think through how to start the story and have even thought about your characters and how they will factor into the plot. Now you'll begin working on how to build your plot. Let's take a look at the process of storyboarding.

STORYBOARDING

Storyboarding is a tool that can be used to arrange a story into a plot. The method is to take a stack of index cards and write a major scene from the story on each. If possible, include the opening scene and the climax or ending scene. In this way the story can be bracketed between the beginning and the end and not wander away. Next, lay the cards out in the sequence you've envisioned for the story. Then stand back and examine the story in terms of the seven steps of plot action and how they relate to the story line. Where does the story and the conflict begin? Where is the crisis and climax? Can the cause and effect of the characters' motivations be seen, and are they in the correct order? By moving the cards around and adding cards as needed, the story line can be manipulated to closely connect to the plot.

A storyboard will clearly illustrate the movement of the plot from the stable ground situation to conflict and then to climax. Some commonly used patterns of movement found in stories include movement from:

- problem to solution
- mystery to solution
- conflict to peace
- danger to safety
- confusion to order
- dilemma to decision
- ignorance to knowledge
- questions to answers

THE THIRTY-SIX DRAMATIC SITUATIONS

These situations were compiled by Georges Polti in the 1800s and were based on earlier work of Carlo Gozzi. Dramatic situations are not plots. They are categories of sources of conflict in a story that can be included in a plot. Most plots combine several of these situations to create the conflict that drives the story. Since Polti created his original list, it has been modified and massaged by many writers, but the essential list remains intact although perhaps renamed. Recently a thirty-seventh situation has been added to the list, which is listed at the end. Listed on the following pages are the dramatic situations with the character types that would normally be associated with the situation.

- **Supplication:** Someone who needs help, usually due to the antagonist

- **Deliverance:** Someone who needs help and someone to rescue that person
- **Vengeance of a crime:** Someone is the avenger and someone else is the criminal
- **Vengeance taken for kin upon kin:** Someone is the avenging kinsman, the guilty kinsman, someone to remember the victim, and a relative
- **Pursuit:** Someone is the fugitive and the pursuer
- **Disaster, vanquished:** Characters include the vanquished power, the victorious enemy, and the messenger
- **Falling prey to cruelty/misfortune:** Characters are the unfortunate and the master
- **Revolt:** Someone is the tyrant and the conspirator
- **Daring enterprise:** Someone is the bold leader and the adversary
- **Abduction:** Someone is the abductor, the guardian, and the victim
- **The enigma:** Someone is the seeker, the interrogator
- **Obtaining:** Characters include the solicitor, the adversary, opposing parties, and the arbitrator
- **Enmity of kin:** Someone is the malevolent kinsman or the hated or hating kinsman
- **Rivalry of kin:** Characters are the preferred kinsman and the rejected kinsman
- **Murderous adultery:** Someone is the adulterers and the betrayed spouse
- **Madness:** Someone is the mad person or the victim
- **Fatal imprudence:** Characters include the imprudent and the victim

- **Involuntary crimes of love:** Someone is the lover, the beloved, and the revealer
- **Slaying of kin unrecognized:** Someone is the slayer or the unrecognized victim
- **Self-sacrifice for an ideal:** Characters include the hero and the person sacrificed
- **Self-sacrifice for kin:** Someone is the hero, the kinsman, or the person sacrificed
- **All sacrificed for passion:** Someone is the lover, the beloved, or the person sacrificed
- **Necessity of sacrificing loved ones:** Someone is the hero or the beloved victim
- **Rivalry of superior versus inferior:** Characters include the superior rival and the inferior rival
- **Adultery:** Characters include the deceived spouse and the adulterers
- **Crimes of love:** Someone is the lover, the beloved, and the victim
- **Discovery of the dishonor of a loved one:** Characters include the dishonorer and the guilty one
- **Obstacles to love:** Someone is lovers and people who stand in their way
- **An enemy loved:** Characters include the beloved enemy, the lover, and the hater
- **Ambition:** Someone is the ambitious person, the adversary
- **Conflict with a god:** Someone is the immortal, the mortal
- **Mistaken jealousy:** Someone is the jealous, the object of jealousy, the supposed accomplice, and the author of the mistake

- **Erroneous judgment:** Someone is the mistaken one, the victim of the error, the author of the error, the guilty person
- **Remorse:** Characters include the culprit, the victim, the interrogator
- **Recovery of a lost one:** Someone is the seeker, the one found
- **Loss of loved ones:** Someone is the kinsman slain, the kinsman spectator, the executioner
- **Mistaken identity:** Characters include the mistaken one, the victim of the mistake, and the author of the mistake

Combining several of these situations will assist an author to develop a plot that will sustain a novel. These dramatic situations can be used to create plot twists, give the reader insight into a character, create a dilemma for the protagonist, create a subplot, form the basis of a scene, or form any other cause-and-effect situation to move the plot toward the climax.

CRITICAL POINTS OF PLOTTING A STORY

When designing a plot, there are a number of critical factors that will directly affect how well the plot works to support the story. If an author has a plot designed, the following ten points will serve as a guide to assess how well the plot may work.

Nothing Happens Randomly

Every element of the story should have significance. If it does not advance the plot, it shouldn't be in the story. Names, places, actions, and events must have a specific purpose to the plot. Unneeded detail slows the pace of the story to a crawl. Young adult readers expect a story to move along quickly and are not interested in literary flourishes or exhibitions of the author's erudition.

The Plot Grows from the Reactions of a Character under Adversity

Once the point of no return has been reached, the plot must proceed based on the characters' reactions to the event, which will set up the next event. At this point the author cannot introduce another chain into the series from another direction or have the protagonist step out of character with a plausible reason.

Each Character Has His Own Urgent Personal Goal

The objective that the protagonist is trying to achieve must be important to that character. At the same time, the author must allow the reader to understand what the character's motivation is that makes that goal so important. In this way the reader can share the emotion of the challenges and successes of overcoming the obstacles that stand in the way of attaining that goal.

The Plot of the Story Is the Sum of Its Individual Characters

In young adult novels the protagonist rarely acts alone. The other characters in the story each have their own agendas, which may conflict with the agenda of the protagonist. In all cases the other characters should influence, more or less, the behavior of the protagonist as he follows his own agenda.

The Plot Begins before the Story

The real story begins at the point of no return. Until then the character has the option of not reacting to the incitement and returning to the stable ground level. Once the point of no return is passed, the character's world has changed forever and he must react to the new situation, propelling him toward the climax.

Important Events Are Foreshadowed

The first part of the plot before the point of no return is a brief look into the future—a teaser for the reader to encourage him to keep reading. The ending of the story should have the elements that were presented to the reader at the beginning. The plot is one long, unbroken chain of interconnected events where initial causes of the protagonist's quest can be seen along the entire length.

Keep in Mind What Sort of Story Is Being Told

All stories are about the relationship of an individual to society. In a comic story an individual is isolated and achieves acceptance through a series of events or creates his own society where he can be integrated and accepted. A tragic story is one in which the protagonist is part of the society and becomes isolated. In either case the plot should keep the reader in suspense until the end. If the reader knows it's a comedy, the exact nature of the climax should be a surprise. On the other hand, if the protagonist is doomed to failure, his downfall should come from a cause the reader already knows about and understands.

The Protagonist Eventually Takes Charge of Events

At the beginning of a story, even for a short time, the protagonist is passive and simply reacting to events. At some point in the story, he should take charge and actively attempt to change the events happening around him. This helps to define the protagonist's character and puts him in the position for more serious conflicts, all leading to the final climax. The plot cannot carry a passive character—the character has to be at the head of the action.

The Plot Dramatizes the Character

The plot is the road map of the story, and every event and the protagonist's response to that event should provide insight into his character. Plot elements provide opportunities for the characters to be brave, stupid, timid, generous, caring, or demonstrate any other human characteristic. This behavior fleshes out the character and makes him three dimensional and more real to the reader.

Ironic Plots Subvert Their Surface Meanings

Ironic plots must be handled carefully, because they can create a situation where the story ending becomes disappointing. Taking a goal that is strongly desired by the protagonist and turning it into a Pyrrhic achievement can be a powerful tool, but with young adult readers it must be an integral part of the ending that can be easily understood.

"!!"

- ADVICE FROM PUBLISHERS ROW -

Phoebe Yeh, vice president and publisher of Crown Books for Young Readers:

"Everyone wants to read a good story. You can't have a good story if the story line doesn't hold up or if the plotting is 'problematic.' When I read manuscripts and books, the writing needs to engage me in some way. If I am considering the story line, it must be interesting, exciting, dramatic. Something about the writing needs to make me want to know what happens next and to make me want to keep on reading. This is not just moving your characters from point A to B to C. The protagonist has to evolve along the way.

"In the tween novel *We Can't All be Rattlesnakes* by Patrick Jennings, Crusher, a gopher snake who is mistaken for a rattlesnake, protests her captivity by developing an unlikely friendship with Breakfast, a mouse, instead of making a meal out of Breakfast. The suspense and the evolving friendship keep the story moving along.

"In the young adult novel *Freaked* by J. T. Dutton, even though his prep school life is falling apart yet again, Scotty Loveletter will not be deterred from the one great passion in his life—his love for the Grateful Dead and his quest of leaving no stone unturned to get to the next Dead concert. Will he or won't he make it? These two novels are examples that do not demonstrate the pitfalls of bad plotting. They are not overwritten. They do not have convoluted plots that don't make sense and aren't logical. The plots do not meander. And they both have a resolution that is believable and satisfying."

CREATING SUSPENSE IN THE PLOT

Maintaining suspense in the plot as the story unwinds is essential to maintain the interest of the reader. This can be accomplished by keeping the reader's anticipation fresh and presenting additional complications and conflict. Each step forward must be met with additional difficulties that will cause the next event. As the protagonist deals with each of these events, one after the other, the events will collectively direct the protagonist to the climax.

The reader must sympathize with what is happening to the protagonist and keep reading to find out what will happen. A careful balance must be maintained between giving the reader too little or too much information so that the final climax can be set up and used to bring the story to a satisfactory end. There are four factors to consider when planning a plot in order to sustain the suspense through the length of the story.

Foreknowledge

The reader must know that something bad is going to happen to one or more of the characters—usually to the protagonist or characters closely associated with him—as a result of conflict. The reader must have a clear idea of what the protagonist faces and may even have knowledge that the character does not have. Over the next chapters of the story, the reader will be given time to anticipate the event and consider possible outcomes before the author shows him exactly what happens.

Uncertainty of the Outcome of the Conflict

Bad things happen to good characters—the resolution of the conflict does not always result in a happy ending. The author must convince the reader that a disastrous outcome may result from a particular conflict, and the more sympathetic the character is to the reader, the more impact negative results will have on the reader. The ticking time bomb of the fate of the protagonist can be completely defused if the reader knows that the author will come up with a plot device to extricate the character.

Coincidences and JITNOT (Just in the Nick of Time) Situations

Odd, unexpected things happen in real life, so they can certainly happen in a story, but they should be used sparingly and with extreme care. An author can get away with an unexpected confluence of events in two situations. The first is when the fact of the coincidence is one of the incitement forces of the story. A chance event sets off a chain reaction of events that leads the protagonist into a conflict that is not resolved until the climax of the story. The second use is when the coincidence makes things worse for the protagonist. A coincidence will seem contrived when it improves the character's situation and should be avoided.

Another, more specific form of coincidence is the JITNOT

situation. The classic JITNOT is the situation where just as the wagon train settlers are about to be wiped out by the Indians, out of nowhere the cavalry rides over the ridge. An author who uses this plot device tells the reader that no matter what happens, he will create a JITNOT to save the character in every situation. From that point on the suspense has vanished, because the reader knows the outcome of the story will be in the protagonist's favor. This is the literary equivalent of the author allowing readers to peek at the answers in the back of the book.

Withholding Information

In any suspenseful situation the reader should know the identity of the character, the point of view of the narration, where the character is and what he is doing, and enough of the background information known to that character so that the reader can understand the character's action. Not providing this information confuses the reader and should not be done unless there is an overwhelming reason. Holding back does not create suspense; it creates annoyance and negatively changes the reader's satisfaction with the story.

PLOTTING FAULTS

Sometimes the plot is not successful, and after the climax the ending of the story is unsatisfactory. Common faults that can cause the plot and, ultimately, the story to fail include the following.

Lack of Growth or Change on the Part of the Characters

One of the defining characteristics of young adult fiction is the change in the characters resulting from the conflict in the story. The plot in all its forms is about how life affects the characters. After the climax, the reader must be able to see that the protagonist (and occasionally other characters) has learned something, grown, or changed in some way that is reflected in his behavior. A reader should be able to look back from the climax and trace the cause and resulting effects that have had an impact on the character. The character must now act differently than he did at the beginning. The author should apply indirection and not tell the reader either through the narration or the voice of the character how the character has changed. "I faced [write a conflict here] as a boy and became a man" is an extremely poor ending and borders on preaching. The character must show that he is different.

Weak Conflict

At the end, does the reader discover that the conflict really wasn't that important after all? The conflict faced by the protagonist must involve a decision that may be ethical, be against his better judgment, affect another character, or in some way cause something terrible to happen if he doesn't attain it. The goal of the character must be something that he wants at all costs and that will have significant effect on the character's world.

Overused Endings

Some endings have been overused and abused so much that they alienate the reader. These include a protagonist who is not what he seems—a girl instead of a boy; the "it was only a dream" ending and its variation in a fantasy novel where the protagonist is dragged back to the real world; and the "everyone lived happily ever after" ending. Few things in life are entirely all good. Tempering a successful ending with a touch of failure adds depth to the ending and causes the reader to stop and pause to consider the theme of the novel.

This is not so say that an author cannot use these endings if he comes up with a unique, interesting variation, but he does it at his own risk.

Lacking in Satisfaction

There are a number of possible sources of this problem. First, the ending is obvious or has been predictable since the beginning. Second, the author has not planned ahead for the ending, which should be the largest, most dramatic climax of the story, and instead has tacked on a weak, irrelevant, or illogical ending. Third, the outcome is not sufficiently important to the characters, or after many pages of buildup the resolution to the problem is trivial. Young adult fiction requires the ending to have a significant impact on the characters to the point where their lives have been changed.

Preaching

Many authors attempt to use their story to make a statement about society, politics, religion, morals, values, and many other ethical areas. This must be handled with great care and under only two circumstances. The first is when the statement to be made is important and far-reaching. Issues such as poverty and racial injustice as handled by Mark Twain and Charles Dickens are good examples. The second is when the point is made by showing it through the interactions of the characters and the setting. An example is the novel *To Kill a Mockingbird* by Harper Lee. The tragedy of racial discrimination is vividly illuminated through the reactions and emotions of Jem and Scout. The reader understands what the author is saying through the eyes of the characters. On the other hand, when an author uses the characters' voices to make his own personal statement, it becomes preaching. At that point the author might as well get out his soapbox, climb up on it, and harangue the reader to convince him of the righteousness of his cause.

Wandering

A meandering story line is a result of the author not having a clear idea of where the plot is going. One solution is to give the protagonist a stronger motivation and increase the difficulty of success. What terrible things will happen to the characters if the conflict is not successfully resolved? A storyboard can improve a wandering plot by helping the author identify the beginning and the end of the story before writing a word. If there is a definite ending in sight at all times, the story line is less likely to veer off track and take unnecessary side trips.

Coincidences and JITNOTs

Coincidences and JITNOT situations are difficult to handle in the body of the story, but they are devastatingly ruinous to a story ending. One reason for this is that the protagonist has devoted his entire effort to dealing with the conflict, only to have the resolution jerked out of his hands by an outside, unexpected force. In young adult literature, an ending like this is too much like having the protagonist's parents show up at the critical point and take care of the problem whether he wants them to or not. A second reason is that the solution to the conflict must come from the internal chain of events that started at the beginning of the novel at the incitement point. If the story is not allowed to progress to its logical conclusion, without external interference, what was the point of the story?

Lack of Focus on the Principal Characters

A story may be confusing with too many characters and subplots and too much action. In young adult fiction, the author must sharply focus on the main character and use subplots and other characters to dramatize and highlight the action of the protagonist.

"!!"

- ADVICE FROM PUBLISHERS ROW -

Wendy Lamb, publisher of Wendy Lamb Books:

"If your secondary characters dilute the focus of the main story because reader feels distracted and can't keep track of them, then you have too many. Tell us a story. Make us keep reading. Be in charge."

Dangling Threads

At the end, all subplots and themes should be wrapped up in a neat package. A reader should never finish a novel wondering what happened to a character or situation that was important at the beginning and now has inexplicably disappeared. Like a surgeon, an author should count all his tools at the end to be sure everything that was used throughout the operation is accounted for at the time he closes.

Deus ex Machina

This Latin phrase describes a plot device that originated in Greek tragedy. When the plot was so hopelessly tied up that no solution seemed possible, a crane lowered actors in a basket (who were usually portraying gods) onto the stage, and they would then straighten everything out, bringing the play to a close. When an author paints his characters into a corner and then a plot device suddenly appears to rescue them, all of the suspense and anticipation is lost. The final solution to the conflict and complications of the protagonist must always arise internally from the previous action of the story. A deus ex machina climax should cause the reader to consider suing the author for storytelling fraud.

Pointless Story

The plot structure looks complete and the characters have resolved the conflict, but the story seems to be rather pointless. This problem occurs when the conflict the protagonist faces is not important enough or does not affect him deeply enough. It can also arise when the reader is not empathizing well enough with the chief characters and, as a result, does not care about the ultimate outcome of the story. These stories are often found in genres where the plot has fossilized into a formula and the author has not spent enough time developing the characters' personalities. If the author does not care deeply about the lives of his characters and how they resolve the conflict, the reader won't either.

When it comes to plot, don't force the issue of uniqueness too much. It's not your plot that needs to be unique, it's your story—remember, story is the overarching sequence of events as the reader imagines them to have taken place, in the order in which they would have occurred in life. Creating a believable chain of events that your characters can react to and struggle against is the key to constructing a memorable plot.

CHAPTER 6

SETTING AND TIMELINE

Everybody, every story, belongs somewhere. Even if setting doesn't play a main role in the story, it's a good idea to have details set in one's own mind. The setting is the stage that your characters work from. So it's important to have a clear vision, whether the place is real or fictitious, because the setting can dictate how the plot develops. The setting can also help set the stage for the conflict in your story. Once you've identified in your mind where to place your characters, you have to make that place known to the reader. Readers don't have access to the characters' environment until you give it to them. Writers can help this process along by asking questions such as, What does my main character's room look like? How big a house does she live in? Does she walk to school or ride the bus? Does she live in the Midwest? On a farm? In the city? These details will find their way into your story and add life to the book. To help you develop the setting for your novel, let's take a look at a few of the essential elements that will help you create it.

SETTING

Setting is the essential foundation of storytelling. Imagine Harry Potter without Hogwarts Castle; Tom Sawyer and Huck Finn without the Mississippi River; or Poe's *Fall of the House of Usher* without its setting.

During the whole of a dull, dark, and soundless day in the autumn of the year, when the clouds hung oppressively low in the heavens, I had been passing alone, on horseback, through a singularly dreary tract of country; and at length found myself, as the shades of the evening drew on, within view of the melancholy House of Usher.

Setting is the time and location of a story—the main backdrop for the action. Some writers use the analogy of a theater stage to define setting, suggesting that characters appear and interact in front of mostly static scenery as the story is told. Unfortunately, these definitions are simplistic and may limit the story.

As in the Poe quotation above, an author must give the reader a sense of the "place" where characters live as early as possible in the narrative. This is sometimes called *milieu*. Place can be defined in three broad aspects:

- **Emotional:** Characters exhibit emotions throughout the story, but the setting can show emotions as well, which is generally referred to as the mood or tone. The mood of the setting tends to operate independent of and without regard to the characters. The calm ocean can become threatening, the clouds can break and a gloomy day can become sunny, and many other changes in physical environment can occur. As a result, they can directly affect or change the emotional state of the characters.

- **Physical, which can be subdivided into man-made and natural environments:** The human-created physical environment includes locations such as rural, urban, a luxurious hotel room, or a Gothic mansion, as well as clothing, vehicles, the character's glasses, type of food he eats, and any other man-made item the character can interact with. Aspects of the natural world are the second subdivision. These tend to be of larger scale and include climate, weather, deserts, mountains, plains, and other types of natural phenomena.

61

- **Cultural/social:** This aspect is complex and can have enormous impact on the characters' behaviors, which will direct the story. The texture of a story will vary dramatically between characters who are different racially, politically, or ethnically, or who have different levels of education, affluence, and many more traits.

Taken together, these three aspects define a character's place in the story. An author may create a global place that is applied to the entire story, or place might be defined for each single scene.

Place is almost always dynamic. Physical environment in particular can change rapidly and affect the action significantly. Cultural settings can change as well simply by moving the character from one geographic location to another. Place can remain static only for a short period of time, even in small settings. For example, a simple setting such as a closed room will change as the result of passing time, which may cause an important change in the action.

The purpose of a setting is to create an environment so that readers can clearly visualize where and when the story takes place. This will anchor the characters in the reader's mind so that the story cannot happen anywhere else at any other time. When a reader recalls the story, he should be able to see the action occurring within the frame of the setting.

In young adult fiction setting can easily be overdone. Many authors delight in writing lengthy phrases and paragraphs of lush, incredibly detailed descriptions of settings. Today's young adult readers, having grown up using the Internet and playing high-speed computer games, will skip those paragraphs and pages of dense prose, flipping ahead to find where the story action starts again—or skip the whole novel. It's best to use only a description of a setting as required at a particular point in the story.

TYPES OF SETTINGS

The three types of settings seem obvious, but many beginning writers have difficulty with them. At all times an author must keep in mind that readers of fiction know that the story is imaginary but still want to experience it as if it were real. Setting is the tool that brings a story to life in the reader's mind. How many millions of young adult readers would like nothing better than to climb onto a broomstick and actually play a game of Quidditch? It's up to the author to create a setting that allows the reader to imagine himself as part of the story.

- **Realistic:** Realistic settings are those entirely based in the real world. All of the physical characteristics of the universe are in place, and characters interact with their environment in totally expected ways. The author cannot take any liberties with the world for any purpose. This not as restrictive as it sounds, however. Among the millions of known places on the earth, under the sea, or in space, there are many interesting places a writer can use that are suitable settings for a story.

- **Fantasy:** Fantasy settings are more or less entirely the creation of the author. These settings range from an entirely imaginary world with its own laws and characteristics such as magic, ESP, and supernatural creatures, and move toward a more realistic setting with some fantastic twists. The most important aspect of a fantasy setting is that it be consistent. All of those points where the characters and the setting interface must be planned in advance. Nothing destroys the magic of a fantasy faster than an arbitrary change in the laws of the world as a plot device.

- **Blended:** A blended setting is a combination of the real world and the author's imagination. There are gradual shadings from a free-form fantasy world and a blended setting. In a blended setting the author uses the real world for most of his settings with some specific, well-defined changes for the story. Most of the time, the reader will see a world that he recognizes and lives in every day. The deviation from the expected norm enhances and emphasizes the magical effects of the story by providing a realistic backdrop for the fantasy.

Planning a Setting

For many authors, the setting of a story is a matter of convenience. A story will be set in a location that the author knows well or that meshes with the theme of the story. To decide where the story should take place, an author should keep in mind that the setting will shape the characters' behaviors because it is always exclusionary. A particular setting will make some actions of the characters possible—and at times inevitable—but at the same time make other actions impossible. A few examples include settings for science fiction, westerns, fantasy, historical fiction, or specific places like rural and urban environments, the oceans, or a tropical jungle.

Because of the inherent limiting factors of any setting, the author should carefully choose his setting before writing the story. Making abrupt changes with a clumsy plot device simply to move characters from one setting to another only to enable the story to continue interrupts the flow and forces the reader out of the story to reassess what is happening. The following are some pointers to use while planning a setting.

Choose the time and place that will best enable the story's flow.

Does the setting allow the characters sufficient freedom to interact with one another and their environments to tell the story as effectively as you wish? All settings have restrictions. Will the restrictions of this setting impede or enhance the story by increasing the conflict?

Consider all the details of what is going on in this setting.

What is happening at that particular time and place? People almost always do more than one thing at a time and interact on many levels. How they do these things will tell the reader a great deal about the personality, occupation, and social status of a character without using exposition.

Determine what makes this setting unique.

No two places in the world are identical. They may have similar characteristics, but the author must look at those things that make a particular setting most useful to his story. How is the difference between Deadwood and Cheyenne or Mars and the moon going to shape the behavior of the characters?

Modify a setting.

Even a real setting does not have to be an exact copy. Small changes in details can create a completely different tone or feel of a location and add depth to the reader's image of the place of the story. Modifications of a real setting will provide more flexibility for action in the story.

Suggest rather than explain the setting.

Limit the use of exposition as much as possible. Lengthy blocks of text with long, adjective-larded sentences present formidable barriers to the abilities and interests of young adult readers, especially at the younger end of the age spectrum. Sketches of a setting where each word has been weighed and tested for its value in describing the scene are much better than exposition. Use the minimum number of words to fire up the young reader's imagination and let him create the image of the setting in his mind. One of the great strengths of fiction is that each reader will see the story his own way. Only the most egotistical writer would demand that his readers see the image as he sees it by writing lengthy setting descriptions.

Include all the senses.

The vast majority of sensory information we receive is visual. Physiologically, that's simply how human perception works, and we can't help it. As a result, settings are frequently created that use only sight and neglect the other four senses. Keep in mind that on the written page all five senses are on equal footings. In planning a setting include the touch of a rough-haired animal, the smell of the pine-covered mountain, the sound of a nearby interstate highway, and the taste of a flat can of root beer. All will contribute to the overall perception of the setting and fix the image in the reader's mind.

Tailor the setting to the length of the scene or story.

The setting is not the story. The shorter the length of the story, the fewer words should be devoted to the description of the setting. But because the story is shorter, each word becomes proportionally more important. Each word of the setting must be chosen to provide the best description of the setting as possible.

The setting as character

Setting can define the interaction between characters by limiting or enabling the action. In certain situations the setting can become a character with independent action, forcing other characters to behave in ways that will advance the plot. An unexpected change in weather, avalanches, fire, and drought are typical examples of a setting taking on the role of a character. In some cases the setting can be anthropomorphized into an almost-human character. In the last book of the Harry Potter series, for example, Hogwarts Castle actively joins the final battle against Lord Voldemort.

Writing Descriptions of a Setting

Okay, so now you have your setting in mind. What things should you include? What things should you not include? What impression do you want to create in the reader's mind? What details will make your setting linger long after the reader has closed your book? What would be the best way to describe this setting? While you're thinking about the answers to these questions, here are some important concepts to keep in mind.

Settings and Scenes

A setting written on a page is not the same as a setting created for a visual medium such as television or film. Visual mediums show every detail, whether they are important to the story or not. Listing details in a room or in a landscape or other setting only because they are there slows the story to a crawl by unnecessarily drawing out a scene. Only those elements of a setting that are essential to that moment in the story should be included. Young adult readers want to slash through the excess verbiage and get to the story. An author must decide which details are essential for the reader to understand the scene and are needed to set up later scenes, and cut everything else.

Florid Descriptions

Long strings of adjectives, similes, metaphors, and dependent phrases are no substitute for short declarative sentences that describe the setting. The author's objective is to link the readers' imagination to his by creating a mutually understood environment. Young adult readers will not connect to the author's imaginary world unless the descriptions are easily accessible to them.

Fitting the Setting into the Story

Many novels are lost in the first few pages when an author tries to list all the characters, their relationships, locations, and interactions in one large data dump. The novel should open with action as soon as possible, but the description of setting and characters should be limited to only what is needed. A university study of the first few pages of a large number of bestselling novels shows that 37 percent began with a detailed setting while 45 percent limited the setting or integrated it into the character's dialogue or narrative. The other 18 percent were a mixture that couldn't be clearly defined. The author of the study concluded that when the setting is based on a shared frame of reference, less text is needed and the reader can focus on the characters and action. Young adult readers want the story to begin immediately with a limited, bare-minimum amount of setting. As the story progresses, more details and characters can be introduced and interwoven into the narrative as needed.

Construction of a Setting

In many cases the author uses a setting he knows well. Some authors set their stories in less familiar locations but learn of the setting through doing research, visiting the site, and discussing the location with others who are knowledgeable. Many fantasy and science fiction novels have a setting that is entirely the creation of the author. There are generally three methods of construction.

Top-Down (Macro to Micro)

In this approach the author begins with a broad overview of what the setting for the entire story will be. From there the setting is broken down as many times as necessary into individual components for specific scenes. The top-down approach is useful because all settings are integrated and tightly bound to one another. The advantage of this method is that the writer can easily see the limitations of the settings of all the scenes, promoting consistency and preventing conflicts later. However, one disadvantage to this approach is that it might be a bit time-consuming.

Bottom-Up (Micro to Macro)

In this approach the author begins by focusing on a small aspect of the setting of an essential scene. This setting is given considerable detail and serves as an anchor for the other settings of the story. As the story progresses, additional settings can be created with less and less detail. The advantage is that the setting can be used immediately without waiting for the rest of the world to be designed. The disadvantage is that huge inconsistencies can appear near the end or climax of the story.

Combination

In this approach the author begins with a loose overview of the story's setting and at the same time selects essential scenes where he describes the setting in great detail. The advantage of this method is that as the author expands the story, he is filling in the details between the beginning scenes and the end using the overview as a guide. One potential disadvantage to this approach is that inconsistencies can often be introduced.

Mapping a Setting

Many fantasy novels include a map indicating the geography and locations of where action takes place. There is some debate about the use of maps as a device to clarify the setting. Is the map being used as a substitute for sharp descriptions of the setting, or is it actually contributing to the reader's understanding of where the story takes place? In Anne McCaffrey's Dragonriders of Pern novels, where the setting is a fantasy world and the action takes place anywhere on that planet, maps are useful to understand distances and the scope of the story. On the other hand, maps that add nothing to advance the plot can be a barrier to the reader, because the map will act as a fence confining the reader's imagination.

Also, if an author does not understand the geologic and climatic conditions that create features such as mountains, deserts, plains, and arctic and temperate areas, he would be wise not to attempt a map. Land features are not arbitrary, and creating a mixture solely on the basis of plot requirements will produce a chaotic jumble of unrelated geographic features.

TIMELINES

An intrinsic part of a setting is time. Unlike the real world, where time runs in only one direction, past to future, an author is in complete control of time in his story. He can speed it up, slow it down, jump forward or backward, or leapfrog over stretches of time to tell the story. Time plus place equals a slice of life where a scene or story occurs.

Crowding and Leaping

Ursula K. Le Guin, author of the Earthsea novels and many other award-winning young adult novels, describes her concept of crowding and leaping as follows.

> [Crowding is]...keeping the story full, always full of what's happening in it; keeping it moving, not slacking and wandering into irrelevancies; keeping it interconnected with itself, rich with echoes forward and backward. Vivid, exact, concrete, accurate, dense, rich: these adjectives describe a prose that is crowded with sensations, meanings, and implications.
>
> But leaping is just as important. What you leap over is what you leave out. And what you leave out is infinitely more than what you leave in. There's got to be white space around the word, silences around the voice. Listing is not describing. Only the relevant belongs.

Crowding a story is essential in young adult novels. For this age group, the story has to move. The young adult reader has an extremely low tolerance for lengthy descriptions of setting, long dialogue, the meditative muse, or philosophical discourse. Absolutely everything that does not move the story forward has to be eliminated. The story doesn't have to have action on every page, but every page must be sharply relevant to the story, interesting, and meaningful to the theme of the novel.

Leaping is skipping from scene to scene over periods of time, leaving out parts that are dull, irrelevant, or unneeded. Alfred Hitchcock once irreverently quipped that his films were just like life with the dull bits edited out. This is leaping, and its function in writing a young adult novel is to keep the story full and alive while moving it toward the climax.

Author-Controlled Time

The fact that an author controls the lives of his characters through the use of time does not give him license to overuse it. Flashbacks, flash-forwards, and foreshadowing are all methods of controlling time and are important tools in telling a story. For the young adult reader, use of these techniques should be limited and inserted in a story when there are no other alternatives. When they are used, great care must be taken to ensure continuity, consistency of characters, and well-defined settings. Readers at the lower end of the young adult age group find multiple flashbacks and other time manipulations difficult to follow. A story that follows a straight timeline from introduction to climax is much preferred over a convoluted, hard-to-follow route.

Developing a Timeline

If a story takes place over a significant amount of time, laying out the timeline on paper is a useful tool that will allow the author to place the characters in the correct setting, pace the story, and identify the essential parts that must be told. The timeline also allows the author to place and rearrange the scenes of the story, much like playing a game of solitaire, to achieve the most impact. It's also a way of identifying those scenes that are weak or not needed in the story.

After you've got your cards laid out on the table, look at the sequence of events you've created. Does it make sense? Do the characters age and reach milestones in a realistic fashion? Consider how your timeline relates to your plot. Does it include all the main climaxes of your plot? Are there any events in the timeline that don't occur in the plot? If so, you might want to consider leaving those out, as they're probably not necessary to your manuscript.

SETTING AS A FOUNDATION

Some authors, especially those who write science fiction, may create stories that span long periods of times, sometimes hundreds or thousands of years. Building a timeline with the settings required for the story will create a believable history and foundation for the story. Over hundreds of years much of the setting will change, but much will remain the same. These similar threads running through time tend to be those aspects of the human condition that bind all fiction together. Many of the conflicts that society had to deal with when men sailed on wooden ships are the same conflicts of the men who sail spaceships between the stars. The setting and timeline provide readers with an anchor in reality that will make a story come alive.

The setting of your novel can be instrumental in shaping your manuscript's tone if you handle it well. Remember the atmosphere you want to create, decide on what details will add the most to the feel you want to convey, and pick your approach. If you keep to those general precepts, your setting will resonate in the readers' memory long after they've finished your book.

CHAPTER 7

TRYING ON POINTS OF VIEW

In fiction the author never tells the story directly to the reader. Instead, he uses an avatar within the world he has created, in the form of a narrator. Where the narrator appears to stand in relationship to the reader as he tells the story is what is known as the point of view.

The point of view (POV) can be one of three forms—first person, second person, or third person—or their variants. Viewpoint can be thought of as a measure of the distance the narrator has from the story. In first person the viewpoint is told from the "I" position, so the viewpoint has a distance of zero because the narrator is the central focus through which all events are experienced by the reader. Second person is told from the "you" position, which makes the reader feel like he or she is a character within the story. Finally, in third person, the narrator is farthest from the action, standing to the side and taking a panoramic view of the scene to describe the action.

The viewpoint and narration make up a delicate construction where a break in consistency can completely lose the reader. Consistent, logical POV will keep the reader immersed in the story and help the reader identify with the characters.

Point of view is a term with two important meanings for a writer: "vantage point" and "opinion." The first requires precise use of technique; the second, passion and artistry. Mastering the use of both meanings is crucial to creating a character and a story the reader will care about.

Let's take a look at the different possible POVs. This will help you determine who should be telling your story and figure out how to approach first-, second-, and third-person narratives.

THIRD PERSON

Ninety percent or more of modern fiction is written in third person, usually in the past tense. This POV uses pronouns such as *he, she, they, their, himself,* and so on. The third-person narrator is invisible and not a character in the story, and serves the reader by showing the feelings and inner thoughts of the characters by describing the actions and the interactions of the characters. Three variations of third-person POV are used.

- **Limited:** This POV is sometimes described as the "over the shoulder" perspective. The narrator tells the story as if he were looking over the shoulder of a character, sometimes called the "viewpoint character." This viewpoint character is often the protagonist, and the narrator follows him or her around for the duration of the story, looking at and describing the same things that the character sees. The narrator may be more observant than the character, but is limited to what that character theoretically could observe.

- **Omniscient:** In this POV the narrator can shift focus among characters with complete knowledge of everyone's thoughts and of events that no single character would know.

- **Objective:** The narrator in third-person-objective shows only what is actually happening without the filter of the protagonist's personality. It does not detail the thoughts of any single character. This POV is generally used to reveal information that the protagonist or other characters don't know or realize. It is rarely used for an entire novel.

Advantages

- Provides the reader with a wide, sweeping view of the story from above.
- The reader can know what happens when the protagonist is not in the scene.
- When the protagonist is interacting with other characters, the reactions of those characters, including their thoughts, can be given to the reader.
- A reader may observe a scene from the perspective of different characters, allowing the reader to understand the scene better than any of the individual characters do.
- The feelings of any character or all characters can be explored as needed.
- The author can use simple descriptions to give the reader information that the main character can't know but that the reader needs to follow the story.
- It can increase suspense since readers will know something is going to happen before the protagonist does.
- It's not necessary to show the POV of all characters equally as long as readers see and understand enough of each character to identify and relate to them.
- It works well with a large cast of characters such as in fantasy novels.
- It can tell the story through the eyes of several equally important characters.
- It allows the reader to see inside the mind of the villain and know the plans he has for the protagonist without the protagonist knowing.

Disadvantages

- A writer must deal with the emotions and feelings of all the characters, not just one.

- Sometimes the focus can scatter as a result of dealing with too many characters' perspectives.
- It is easy to lose the reader among shifting POVs in a scene or chapter.
- Poor use of third-person-omniscient POV can make the reader feel unconnected to the characters.

FIRST PERSON

This POV uses first-person pronouns such as I, my, or me to tell the story through the eyes, emotions, and experiences of a single character. In first person the narrator is a character in the story. As a character, the narrator takes part in the action, has opinions, makes judgments, and shows biases. However, the narrator must follow all the rules of being a character. For the narrator to know anything, he must experience it with his own senses or be told about it by another character. The narrator cannot interject his own thoughts into the story.

There are a number of variations to first-person POV.

- **Protagonist/Subjective:** In this POV the reader is told the story through the main character's narration. This is the most popular variation of the first-person POV.
- **Witness:** Unlike the first-person-protagonist POV, the first-person-witness involves a secondary character who narrates the main character's story as he observes the events occurring.
- **Collective:** The story is told in this POV by a group of characters acting as a group using the we pronoun.
- **Reteller:** This POV involves a character narrating the story as he has heard it secondhand.
- **Objective:** The first-person-objective is used most commonly in nonfiction writing such as newspapers or magazines and is seldom used in fiction.

Advantages

- The reader can develop an intimate relationship with the viewpoint character that can provide insight that would not be apparent to the other characters.
- A writer can create a unique, easily identifiable voice and personality for the viewpoint character, since he will spend most of his time with that character.
- The first-person POV allows the writer a greater focus on the feelings, opinions, and perceptions of a single character and how they affect the other characters.
- It allows the narrator's character to be developed by the style of how he tells the story.
- First-person narratives are the easiest to follow, because the POV does not jump between characters.
- This POV can transmit to the reader a greater sense of urgency in a scene.

Disadvantages

- In first person the reader knows, sees, and understands only what the viewpoint character knows. He cannot enter the mind of any other character.
- The author can inadvertently speak with his own voice instead of with the viewpoint character's voice.
- In first person the author must focus on the character's behavior to tell what is happening in the story.
- The author may not be comfortable with the character's actions in a scene, making the scene less effective.
- At times the author will be forced into a POV change or an awkward plot device to relay to the reader what is happening in the story that is beyond the reach of the first-person viewpoint character.
- First-person POV can make unfolding and revealing motivations of other characters difficult.

SECOND PERSON

This POV is a method of narration where the narrator speaks to the protagonist usually in present tense using the pronoun *you*. This is rarely used except in electronic role-playing games and chapter books where the reader chooses the direction of the plot or ending. For example:

"You have to get into the old house. If you choose to go through the window, go to page 10. If you choose to force the door open, go to page 20."

Advantages

- Second person is useful for interactive fiction and in children's picture books.
- It is sometimes used in a story for a series of imperative statements to a character.
- It works best in nonfiction.

Disadvantages

- Writing in second person can produce a story that is slow, clumsy, and difficult to read.
- Constant use of the word *you* creates a situation where the reader feels as though he is being addressed by the author and not the characters.
- The narrator draws attention to himself instead of the characters.
- It does not allow for empathy to develop between characters and the reader.

- AUTHOR WORKING -

Lauren Baratz-Logsted, bestselling author of books for kids, teens, and adults:

"A character arises out of incident. I start with an idea.

"My own pregnancy gave me the idea for *Angel's Choice*, a serious YA book about a high school senior fast-tracked for Yale who discovers she's pregnant. There might have been reports about teen pregnancy. I started thinking about my own life and girls who got in, quote, 'trouble.' And I started writing the story. I didn't set out to write a YA novel, but then I started to realize, this is an authentically teen voice. It's very present tense and immediate. YA books often give readers the impression that the author is saying: I am here now. The present tense often works. Teens want to feel it's happening now. Not all the time and with every genre, of course."

PICKING THE RIGHT VIEWPOINT CHARACTER

The viewpoint character is the character through whom the story is told. Often a writer will assume that only first person requires a viewpoint character, but third-person narration requires a viewpoint character as well. The perceptions of the senses and feelings of the viewpoint character will shape the reader's experience of the action in the story. It also allows for contrasting emotions, since one character may view the same scene differently from all other characters in the story.

In adult novels the viewpoint character can change from one scene or chapter to the next. This allows the reader to see the world created by the author through the eyes of more than one person, strengthening the understanding of the plot. In young adult fiction it's better to stay with a single viewpoint character, usually the character who is most impacted by the story. This allows the reader to develop a more sympathetic, personal relationship with the character.

Many writers assume that the viewpoint character should be the protagonist. This is often the case, but it doesn't have to be. The viewpoint character should be the person through whose eyes the reader will see the majority of the action. Third person may work best if there is no compelling reason for a character to personally tell the reader the story. On the other hand, the story of a character whose unique beliefs, opinions, desires, judgments, and hopes color the story should be told in first person.

There are five major considerations when selecting a viewpoint character.

- **The character should be sympathetic to the reader.** The viewpoint character is a filter through which thoughts, feelings, and actions are translated to the reader. A character whom a reader can't build a positive emotional bond with will not be able to successfully carry a story. Choose the POV that will communicate this emotional attachment to the reader most effectively.

- **The viewpoint character must be present the majority of the time.** It would be counterproductive to select a viewpoint character who will miss most of the action of the story. This would force the story to be mostly told through third-person narration instead of first. While occasionally shifting from first to third person in a story is acceptable, if most of the story needs to be told in third person because the viewpoint character is absent, the entire story should probably be told in third person.

- **The viewpoint character must be actively involved in the story and not a chance observer.** It's not enough that the viewpoint character be present; the character must be a major player in the action. If the viewpoint character is carrying the load of the story and plot, it is generally a first-person POV or limited-third-person POV.

- **The viewpoint character should have a personal stake in the outcome of the conflict.** The outcome of the story must be important to the viewpoint character even if the outcome depends on another character's action. In both first- and third-person POV an emotional commitment to the conflict is needed by the viewpoint character.

- **The viewpoint character should have the longest story arc.** A story arc is a plot that is resolved within the pages of the story. There should be a long main plotline that may include several shorter subplots. The viewpoint character's story arc should be the main plotline rather than the subplots of the other characters. If the subplots are numerous and important, the story would be best told in third-person-omniscient POV.

Once a viewpoint character has been chosen, an author should firmly establish the position of the character in the story. As soon as that character appears in the story, the reader should be introduced to his emotions, thoughts, and intents or motivations in order to establish a connection as early as possible.

Changing Points of View within a Story

A general rule is to use the same POV throughout a story, or at least use changes only when absolutely needed to advance the plot. The novel by E. L. Konigsburg *The View from Saturday* uses a changing point of view by effectively moving from the first-person viewpoint character to third person when a different perspective of the action is needed.

- ANATOMY LESSONS -

Jacqueline Woodson, Caldecott and National Book Award winner:

"I think all point of views work—if the writer has a good handle on why they are using whichever one they choose. With my novel *If You Come Softly*, I write in first person for Ellie and third person for Jeremiah. This is an obvious choice—Ellie has lived to tell the story and Jeremiah hasn't. So I wouldn't be able to put Miah's in first person—he's dead. I spent a lot of time rewriting that book because for a long time I didn't know Miah was going to die. So it was in two first-person POVs, then first and second person. In *Behind You* I think Miah is always in second person—'You do not die. Your soul steps out of your body'—because he's dead and he's talking about all of us, bringing the reader in to share this experience of dying and the after-death."

THE UNRELIABLE NARRATOR

Imagine being told a story by someone whose version of events just didn't seem to match up with things as you saw them. Perhaps you felt that person was skewing things to fit his perspective—or maybe he wasn't that perceptive. How were you supposed to know the truth? Enter the unreliable narrator.

Sometimes the narrator may not be telling the truth or is telling the truth about an event from his own skewed point of view. The credibility of the narrator comes into question as a result of psychological instability, powerful bias, lack of knowledge or understanding, or even lying to deliberately mislead the reader. Unreliable narrators are usually first-person narrators, but third-person narrators can be unreliable, too.

Some would argue that in young adult literature all narrators are unreliable. The young protagonist and other young characters often lack the experience and emotional and psychological maturity to relate an event accurately, particularly one with a high emotional value. A young teen protagonist will exhibit adult personality characteristics and at the same time retain many aspects of childhood behavior. These would include outright lying, exaggerations, flights of fantasy, and imaginary beliefs, although a clearly identified dream scene is not considered an example of an unreliable narrator. In Mark Twain's *Adventures of Huckleberry Finn*, Huck's inexperience leads him to make unreliable judgments about other characters in the story.

Unreliable narration, particularly by a first-person narrator, can add insight to the character's personality and provide plot twists and satisfying revelation endings. It also forces readers to reconsider how they experience the story, especially their sympathies for the protagonist.

"!!"

- ADVICE FROM PUBLISHERS ROW -

Wendy Lamb, publisher of Wendy Lamb Books:

"The right POV is the one that allows the author to tell the story in the most compelling and believable way. It unlocks the author's deepest, most useful and fruitful sources for the idea.

"Sometimes the author writes a draft in one POV and the story isn't working. Trying the next draft in a different POV can be very helpful. If that second POV feels more natural, then it's the one to use. If it also feels wrong, that can help clarify problems in the story that need to be resolved. Perhaps the wrong character is the narrator!"

COMMON POV PROBLEMS

- **Changing the POV for no particular reason.** Changing the POV must be done only to tell the story more effectively. Arbitrary changes will distract the reader and break the flow of the story.

- **Shifting the POV too many times.** There are times in a story when it's necessary to change the point of view. These changes should be made only as required. In a story told in first person, the POV may briefly change to third person for a short time while the character is not in a scene.

- **Changing the viewpoint character in a scene.** When the viewpoint character changes in a scene, it becomes difficult to know who is speaking or who is taking part in the action. A viewpoint change should take place at a chapter break.

- **Beginning a scene without establishing the viewpoint immediately.** When a viewpoint change takes place, it's essential that the reader know as soon as possible, to maintain the continuity of the story.

- **Allowing the viewpoint character to use a physical sense in an impossible way.** With the exception of the third-person-omniscient point of view, each point of view restricts what each character can know and understand about the story. In first person a character can't know his face turned red from embarrassment unless he is looking in a mirror.

- **Allowing the viewpoint character to experience the thoughts or intent of a non-viewpoint character.** Other characters cannot know another character's thoughts directly. They have to be implied or suggested by the behavior of the other character.

Remember, point of view is both the vantage point from which your novel is told and an opinion. What point of view is going to add the most impact to your story? Once you know this, start planning how you will blend it in with your characters—for example, if using first-person narrative, think about how your character's voice will affect how the reader perceives the novel's events. Consider how you want to use point of view to shape character and direct the reader's feelings about the plot.

CHAPTER 8

LEARNING TO WRITE DIALOGUE

Dialogue is the star of a young adult novel. It stands center stage in the spotlight and brings characters to life. It's the language of a story spoken by the characters to one another but overheard by the reader. A character's dialogues should create an image in a reader's mind so that he can watch the action of the story unfold.

Think of dialogue as a direct window into the character's mind. Someone's language reflects how he thinks. Use dialogue in your novel to display your characters' personalities and make them stand out to your audience.

DIALOGUE ESSENTIALS

Dialogue is when two or more characters in a novel talk directly to one another. That may sound a lot like a conversation; however, dialogue is not conversation.

In any story, when two or more characters come together they communicate with each other, and usually that communication is in the form of talk. But dialogue between characters is not at all like real conversation between people. (If anyone doubts this, go to www.whitehouse.gov and read a verbatim transcript of any news conference.)

In normal conversation:

- People do not talk in complete sentences all the time.

- Long, complex sentences are almost never used except in formal speech.
- People do not use proper grammar.
- Conversation involves give-and-take between people.
- The give-and-take is not smooth and consists of starts and stops with many speech hesitations such as, "uh," "well," "you know," and other similar sounds and expressions.
- Conversation often contains widely differing emotional levels.
- People often interrupt each other.
- Rarely do people discuss things they already know.
- People often do not or cannot say exactly what they mean.
- People exaggerate and outright lie.
- Endless, banal chatter is boring.
- Silence is an important part of conversation.
- Repeatedly saying a person's first name is never done except in extreme emotional situations.
- People's voices have a distinctive timbre and sound.
- Body language used during conversation reflects people's emotions and is an important part of communication.

A writer has to take all of these factors into consideration to create dialogue that is not true conversation but still sounds like conversation to the reader. Every writer finds dialogue difficult to write well at times. The reason for this is that dialogue is at war with itself, trying to achieve mutually exclusive goals. On one hand, it has to sound like clear and understandable conversation between characters, but at the same time it can't be the "real" conversation used in day-to-day communication between people.

Good dialogue often has subtext. It shows the characters' surface interactions, and at the same time it often carries a subtext of what the character has not said that is also important. The subtext gives good dialogue much of its meaning and power. For example, consider the following eight-word line of dialogue.

A fourteen-year-old protagonist sits down in a restaurant. A waitress comes over, hands him a menu, and asks, "What can I get for you today, hon?"

On the surface, it's a question a reader would expect a character to hear in a restaurant. The unspoken subtext, however, is much more complex. Those eight words allow the reader to visualize and learn a great deal about the characters and the setting. The waitress is not working in an upscale, three-star restaurant. She is a working-class woman who likes people and works in a small diner or greasy-spoon truck stop. The protagonist may not be a fast-food junkie and likes eating in a little more formal setting, but not too formal, or there may not be a fast-food joint in his town.

Compelling, effective dialogue with its accompanying subtexts can be identified by asking these questions.

- **Does the dialogue belong to the characters?** A character should be able to freely express himself in a way that reflects his personality. Age, education, experience, and upbringing help define a character's dialogue.

- **Does it sound natural, but not too natural?** The character's speech should have a flowing, smoothly executed rhythm to it that does not draw attention to the dialogue. If the reader has to struggle through the character's speech, he will drop out of the story unless that speech is a part of the character's personality—for example, Hagrid in the Harry Potter series.

- **Does the dialogue have a point?** Each line of dialogue should have a purpose and should not be idle chatter to fill a space. People commonly do this when they make small talk, but it should never be used in fiction, because it can really slow the story down.

- **Does the dialogue use attribution only when it's needed?** The writing should not have extraneous dialogue tags that are not absolutely necessary.
- **Does the dialogue present the voices of the characters so that the reader can distinguish between them?** Each character should be "heard" by the reader as a distinct voice. A character's vocabulary, grammar, timbre, pitch, and so on, all make up the vision of the character in the reader's mind.
- **Does the character's dialogue fit within the scene?** The environment and setting work together to change the character's dialogue. These things are important, but don't overdo it. Less is more. Give the reader enough to visualize the scene and move on.
- **Do the characters communicate at different levels?** Not all people have the ability to express their ideas as well as others. This lack of ability can help define a character's personality. Characters frequently fail to communicate at all, which can create conflict that will add depth to a plot.

PURPOSE OF DIALOGUE

The purpose of dialogue is far more than putting words in a character's mouth to tell a story. A line of dialogue is an ambassador that works on behalf of the character. Dialogue should:

- **Create and develop conflict in the story.** Unlike young adult novels written even fifteen years ago, readers want to see and become involved with the conflict of the story immediately. There is simply no time for a leisurely development of the plot and detailed introduction of characters. Readers want to know what terrible things are looming ahead of the characters not resolved right up front. The characters' dialogue must start out the story fast, keep to the point, and keep the plot moving to the conclusion of the story.

- **Convey the emotions of the characters, express feelings, share experiences, build trust, and create a bond between the character and the reader.** The reader must sympathize with the character by understanding the character's situation and identifying his own position in life with that of the character.
- **Advance the plot.** The reader wants to follow the plot.
- **Set the scene.** Dialogue can help reveal the world in which the characters are living. You can often tell the setting by words or phrases the characters use. For example, you should be able to tell if the characters are in the South or the Northeast.
- **Provide character development.** Dialogue reveals the personality of your characters. Their personalities should reflect in the sound of their dialogue. A nervous character might speak in short, incomplete sentences and rush over other characters' dialogue. An adult will speak with longer, more formal sentences and a larger vocabulary than a twelve-year-old character.
- **Present exposition.** Carefully chosen dialogue will pull the reader into the story by having the characters share their knowledge of their lives and situation with the reader. This dialogue is frequently overdone and becomes too long. The objective is to give the reader only as much as he needs to become part of the story and no more. There will always be time for more exposition later.
- **Break up long blocks of narrative and manage white space.** Large blocks of unbroken text present a formidable, brooding, threatening countenance toward young adult readers of all ages. Ask a school librarian how junior high school kids select books to read for required book reports. Use of dialogue with its shorter sentences opens up thick blocks of text on the page by providing white space. The shorter lines of dialogue are easier to read and understand, and they allow the story to move along quickly.

MECHANICS OF WRITING DIALOGUE

Given how close dialogue is to conversation, it might seem like the easiest thing in the world. It isn't. So here's a quick guide to the technical aspects of writing dialogue.

Dialogue Punctuation

Few rules in writing are as inflexible as dialogue punctuation rules. Any beginning writer who strays from accepted use does so at his own peril. An author struggling with dialogue punctuation can find many guides on the Web as well as in books and magazine articles. Learning the rules, however, does not necessarily mean an author can apply them when he's sitting at the keyboard. The best way to conquer dialogue challenges is to find one or two novels written by successful authors in your genre who use a lot of dialogue. Examine how their dialogue is written and follow the patterns they use. You will have an entire novel demonstrating correct structure and usage.

"!!" - ADVICE FROM PUBLISHERS ROW -

Cecile Goyette, executive editor at Blue Apple Books:

"E. R. Frank's books certainly impressed me in this regard [dialogue]. And Laurie Halse Anderson, Patricia Reilly Giff, and Walter Dean Myers certainly have an impressive grasp of this element. That said, I don't think YA literary dialogue necessarily has to be ultra-similar to real-life contemporary speech to be effective. Very stylized dialogue that doesn't sound like people actually talk or talked can convey persona, plot, and psyche in unique and enjoyable ways—like a particular form of music or poetry."

Andrea Pinkney, vice president and executive editor at Scholastic:

"The strongest writers are those who write every single day. Like Rocky Balboa sprinting the steps of the Philadelphia Museum. The serious writer is one who focuses on his or her own achievements and will strain heart, muscles, and nerves to get to the top."

Kat Brzozowski, associate editor at Thomas Dunne Books/St. Martin's Press:

"For dialogue, read it or say it out loud to someone else, like a script. People talk very differently than writers write. It can be difficult to capture that authentic teen voice, without it sounding like a caricature of a teenager. Sometimes teens like to read about people that are smarter than them. That's why I think someone like John Green does so well, his characters sound so witty and smart. Erring on the side of dialogue that's sounds natural as an adult is sometimes better than failing to capture how teenagers actually talk."

Internal Dialogue

When a character is talking to himself and speaking his exact thoughts, they should be formatted the same as spoken dialogue. If the character is paraphrasing his ideas, italics can be used.

Dialogue Tags

These are identifiers, also known as speech tags, tag lines, or attributions, that are used to tell the reader which character is speaking, vary the pace of conversation, describe the "sound" of the speaker, and add some simultaneous action. This seems to be straightforward usage, but many writers have difficulty with dialogue tags. Improper use or overuse of dialogue tags can easily ruin a great story and mark an author as a rank tyro. Problems with dialogue tags fall into four categories.

Said Bookisms

The word *said* is the Clydesdale workhorse of most dialogue tags and does most of the work in any novel. "Said bookisms" are an author's attempt to substitute an artificial, literary verb to avoid using the word *said* in a dialogue tag. The term was invented at a science fiction writers conference where the writers collected all the alternates for "said" into a fictitious book. From there, the terms "said bookisms" or "bookisms" have passed into general use. Said bookisms include dialogue tags such as these.

"*Up against the wall,*" *snarled the cop.*
"*I didn't do it,*" *he squeaked.*

The list of said bookisms is extensive, but some commonly used terms include *retorted, hissed, smirked, barked, frowned, laughed, sneered, demanded, replied,* and on and on. (The gold standard for over-the-top said bookisms is a character who "ejaculates" a line of dialogue.) Some said bookisms are impossible. How can a character "frown," "grin," or "grimace" his dialogue?

A writer will argue that "said" is boring and that by using bookisms he can add color and interest to his work. The author is half-right. "Said" is boring, but that's why it's used. The dialogue tags should disappear into the background of the story. "Said" becomes invisible so that the reader can focus on the dialogue and the narrative of a scene. Bookisms are speed bumps. When a reader encounters one, he is thrown out of the story and has to reboot his imagination to return to the scene. They also add an unrealistic, often exaggerated, melodramatic tone to a scene, reducing the impact of the story. The key is to make sure the reader can hear your characters speak the emotions and to not have the author tell the reader what the emotions are. I encourage writers to use bookisms sparingly.

Tom Swifties

These are adverbs attached to the verb in a dialogue tag in an effort to emphasize some emotion contained in the dialogue. They are adverbial puns named after the Tom Swift adventure books written at the turn of the twentieth century, which frequently abused dialogue tags. Here are two examples:

> *"The temperature is going down,"* Tom *said coolly.*
> *"I need a pencil sharpener,"* *said Tom bluntly.*

Excessive use of adverbs in dialogue tags is a symptom that the narrative leading up to the dialogue and the dialogue itself are not conveying the emotion of the scene to the reader and should be rewritten.

Too Many Dialogue Tags

Not every line of dialogue has to have a tag. If the characters have distinctive voices and personalities that are reflected in their speech and if the author includes the characters' action, dialogue tags are often not needed.

The Slender Yellow Fruit Syndrome

In journalism it's not uncommon to see the following: "Bill asked John if he wanted an apple or a banana. John chose the slender yellow fruit." In fiction it's called the Burly Detective syndrome, where the author will write: "The Burly Detective spun on his heel as he drew his gun." And of course for all the ladies it becomes the Raven-Haired Beauty syndrome. In all cases, it's an unnecessary aversion to repeating a word—particularly if it's a character name—in the same line, paragraph, or even page. Instead of using a perfectly serviceable, understandable name or pronoun, a writer will create more and more outlandish references to a character's physical appearance or personality to avoid repetition. This is generally counterproductive and creates dialogue where the reader becomes more interested in the next substitution the author has come up with than the story.

Some authors will go for a dialogue tag-misuse trifecta and score a win, place, and show in the same dialogue tag.

"Don't anyone move," growled the Burly Detective menacingly.

Poor use of dialogue tags, bookisms, and Tom Swifties is a symptom of deeper, more significant problems with the scene and the dialogue of the characters. To solve dialogue tag problems, consider:

- Cutting the dialogue tag completely.
- Changing a bookism to *said*.
- Converting the tag into a new sentence.
- Describing an action or the scene so that it expresses the emotion of the tag.
- Strengthening the dialogue and preceding narrative so that the line of dialogue will stand on its own.

The Data Dump

Exposition is essential to almost every story. At some point the reader has to be brought into a setting, which often includes descriptions of the scene, time frame, situation, or characters. To accomplish this, writers will use a line of dialogue that begins "As you know, Sarah…" and wanders sometimes for pages, dumping an avalanche of details on the reader. This is particularly notable in fantasy novels where an entire world that is unknown to the reader must be described and explained. In science fiction the data dump dialogue will often begin with the words "So tell me again, professor…"

Character Changes

This is also known as the "I went into the [pick your favorite adventure situation] as a boy and came out a man." A character should never utter this line of dialogue about himself unless he is being sarcastic or facetious. Young adult readers will recognize the false bravado of the statement instantly. It's extremely rare that a preteen or early teenage character will be psychologically mature enough to have this sort of introspection. He might be able to see it dimly in another character, but would not be able to recognize such a change in himself—let alone talk about it to the reader.

An important, common theme found in young adult literature is coming of age. But in most cases the protagonist may not be aware of the change and will not be able to acknowledge it. The writer must show the change with how the protagonist's dialogue is spoken, how he acts, and how he interacts differently with the other characters such as family members, friends, teachers, and so on.

Show, Don't Tell

This is a common mantra, especially at writers conferences. Generally what's meant is to portray the scene to the reader from a character's perspective with dialogue and action (show) instead of as a narrative summary (tell). In spite of how often it's said, "show, don't tell" is not a particularly rigid writer's rule. A narrative summary can be useful to:

- Vary the pace, rhythm, tone, and texture of a story or scene.
- Avoid unnecessary detailed repetition if a story has many similar action scenes.

- Make a particularly vivid scene stand out between narratives and give it more impact.
- Cut the number of words in a story.
- Quickly move through plot developments that are simply not important enough to justify a scene.
- Leapfrog over blocks of time or distances between scenes that do not need detailed descriptions.

TECHNIQUES OF DIALOGUE STYLE

Young adult fiction is not adult fiction with shorter sentences. Young adult readers are not psychologically, physically, emotionally, or socially mature and do not have the same life experiences as adults. The words an author puts into the mouth of a teenage character must be the words that a person of a certain age might use in order to create realistic dialogue.

Saint Paul said, "When I was a child, I spoke as a child." Similarly, characters who are young adults must speak like young adults. Their words need to reflect the mind-set and vocabulary of their age and situation.

Age-Appropriate Vocabulary

If an author is not familiar with the standard English vocabulary shared by young adult readers, he should spend some time examining it. There are several books and web pages listing and discussing vocabulary for children's age groups. An author can buy grade-level spelling and reading books in many bookstores that will give him insights into what children know at certain ages. A general rule of thumb is that if an author can't find a particular word in a general-circulation local newspaper, young adult readers probably won't know it.

Slang

Using a lot of slang in dialogue may give the character a current popular culture sound, but too much slang can create problems. The meanings of slang words and the words themselves change rapidly and frequently. What is a common slang word today may have disappeared entirely by the time the novel comes out, therefore dating the book. Also, while it may seem to be widespread, slang may be only local or regional. A teen living in California will certainly use different words than one living in Oklahoma. Some of those meanings may be obscene or unsuitable for a young adult audience. Slang should be used extremely sparingly.

Text-Messaging Abbreviations

Most of the issues that arise in dealing with slang apply to text messaging. It too is a moving target for an author. However, there are web pages that define text-messaging abbreviations to help with creating text-message dialogue. As with slang, text messages can be used sparingly, incorporating the most obvious abbreviations that seem to have stood the test of time such as LOL and emoticons such as :) and similar expressions.

Strong Verbs

The same verb used again and again in a scene will squash it flat, forcing out any excitement or anticipation that the characters are trying to express. A good thesaurus is a useful tool to find common verbs to use in dialogue. Keep in mind that there are almost no words that are true synonyms. Almost all words in English have shadings of meaning that can help define a character's personality and show the emotion of a scene. A character can walk across a room, or he can shuffle, skip, crawl, stroll, strut, or march. He can also sidle, perambulate, mosey, or saunter. Don't dive into a thesaurus looking for another word for "walk" just because it has been used too often. Select verbs that match the character's mood and situation, which will add depth to the scene.

The Verb *To Be*

The most commonly used form of this verb in fiction is *was*. It's a perfectly good verb, but it's not a strong verb, and it can be abused. Examine instances where any *to be* verb is used to determine if a stronger, more visual verb can be used instead. This may require that a line of dialogue or narrative be rewritten.

A common form of abuse of the verb *to be* is when it's used with a gerund (an -*ing* word). Here are several examples.

> Joanna said, "I saw the UFO as I was running down the street."
> Joanna said, "I saw the UFO as I ran down the street."
> "The telephone was ringing and I answered it."
> "The telephone rang and I answered it."

Tense

Keep dialogue in a scene in the same tense except where the character is specifically discussing an event in the past or future. In a lengthy scene it's easy to slip and have characters change tense in dialogue. This is especially true in first-person narratives. When exactly does the scene take place? Stick with that tense.

Adjectives and Adverbs

Mark Twain said to search for adjectives and stomp them out. Not every noun has to have an adjective, and not every verb has to have an adverb. In fact, if the narration and dialogue are strongly written using powerful verbs, nouns and verbs can certainly stand alone. Larding dialogue with hoards of adjectives and adverbs only slows the pace of the story and dims the action. Remove an adjective or an adverb and read the sentence again. Was it absolutely essential for the meaning? If not, cut it.

That is not to say you should never use modifiers. Modifying strong nouns and verbs is sometimes necessary to better define them so that they will fit the scene. Colors, size, speed, and similar qualities can be assigned to nouns and verbs that will add to a scene. However, modifiers with indeterminate meanings, such as *very, some, mostly, almost*, and so on, can take meaning away from nouns and verbs. Used in prepositional phrases, these modifiers can become qualifiers and soften the meaning of an entire line of dialogue. Don't have a character constantly waffle. Write with strong nouns and verbs, selecting modifiers that will contribute to a character's speech to make it sharper and clearer.

Talking Heads

Characters rarely sit motionlessly talking to one another. They are almost always in motion when they talk. They use hand and facial gestures, cross their legs, pull on an earlobe, wiggle in their seats, look around the room, clean their glasses, greet other people, whittle on a stick, tap their feet, pop their gum, and on and on. Adding action to the dialogue will show emotional states and provide an opportunity to define a character based on his behavior in conversation.

Figuratively Swinging for the Fences

Be extremely careful with literary fiction; it will often not interest the average young adult reader. Soaring flights of literary erudition will bore the teen reader, who wants to get into the action as quickly as possible. Young adult fiction is characterized by short, declarative sentences in the narration and dialogue and sparse scene descriptions with no extraneous words. The story has to move forward at a brisk pace. Young adult readers do not want to be dazzled with scene descriptions such as:

She turned her face quickly to and fro, gasping for air, but the roric space was thick like a being, like a creature covered all over in fur, so that Afeni fell to the ground in order to escape the gait of her cloying silhouette and of that murky air.

Narrative like that will cause most young adult readers to start paging ahead to find a place where the story gets exciting again, or put the book down.

Echoes

An echo is the same dialogue inadvertently used again somewhere else in the story. Through the editing process or simply because the writer forgot he'd written it, a character will say the same dialogue again (and again) in different words. Sometimes the dialogue may be identical in both cases. These echoes are often not easy to find, but fortunately they tend to appear fairly close to each other in the same scene or a closely related scene. In young adult novels it is not necessary to repeat information to the reader multiple times, no matter how important it may seem to the author. Trust your readers; they got it the first time.

Narrator Intrusion

Sometimes this is called "breaking through the fourth wall." The author, using the voice of the narrator, forces his way into the story, overrides all the characters, and talks directly to the reader. This sort of dialogue can be identified with a POV change. First-person narration by a protagonist uses first-person pronouns such as I, me, my, mine. Third-person narration uses he, his, and theirs. Author intrusion is almost always second person and uses you and your to address the reader. Keeping a tight rein on which point of view the author is using can prevent this.

Clichés

Avoid these words and phrases like the plague. (See why?) Nothing sends a manuscript to the recycling bin faster than a story loaded up with stale, hackneyed phrases, especially when they are found on the first few pages. If an author has a fresh and exciting story and plot, he should use fresh and exciting words to write it. There are several books that have clichés organized in dictionary format as well as web pages listing them—useful tools for a beginning author.

Don't recycle a cliché by turning it around, reversing the meaning, or substituting the nouns. No matter what you think of it, an agent or editor will be turned off by it. Worse yet, some authors will announce a cliché in advance with a line of dialogue that begins like this: "As the old cliché [saw, adage, saying] goes, [insert putrid cliché here]." A line of dialogue like that serves the function of letting the reader know it's time to put the manuscript down.

Misplaced Modifiers

For unintentional humor in a story, nothing beats a misplaced modifier. Here is an example from a young adult novel published in the UK.

> "Suddenly the phone rang. Jamie jumped out of his skin. Miss Crowe took it, and immediately handed it to him."

One hopes that Miss Crowe handed Jamie his skin; he might need it later. The author scored a twofer in this paragraph. He led with a cliché and followed up with a misplaced modifier. Misplaced modifiers are usually artifacts of the editing process where phrases and sentences are being moved around without checking to see if the editing has changed the meaning of words or phrases that come before or after.

Sometimes misplaced modifiers are difficult to spot, since the author knows what he is trying to say and may not misinterpret the sentence the way a reader would. It's always best to have someone else read the manuscript with a critical eye. The members of one writers group tally misplaced modifiers in one another's work. At the last group meeting of the year each member reads the best of his collection.

Rhythm
A character's dialogue can be written so that it has rhythm and cadence, which can help define his personality. Think about a character's personality. Is it quick, perky, slow, suspicious, lighthearted, serious, cheerful, or gloomy? These personality quirks can be written into his dialogue and separate one character's speech from another.

Humor
Humor in dialogue can lighten a scene considerably. But with few exceptions, don't go for belly-laughs. A smile works just as well or better. Humor derived from the situation the character finds himself in works best, because it will never be outdated or misunderstood as time passes. Avoid tricks and gimmicks, contrived situations, forced witticisms, and things that the author thinks should be funny.

The Sixth-Grade-Boy Giggle Test
At the lower end of the young adult age group are children in upper elementary school. Their sense of humor and what they find amusing is enormously different from that of high school–age young adult readers. Double entendres, noisy bodily functions, bathroom/outhouse references, and things that are just "gross," such as snot and boogers, are the height of fifth- and sixth-grade

boys' humor. They will quickly hone in on any and all of these in a novel, whether the author intended them to be interpreted that way or not. They will underline these passages and pass them around to all their friends in study hall, trying unsuccessfully to hold their giggling in. If in doubt, find a sixth-grade boy and have him read the passage in question while observing the color of his face. Chameleons don't change colors that fast. No sixth-grader handy? Ask an upper elementary-grade teacher. They know.

Geographic Locations and Stereotypes

Many young adult novels take place in times and locations that are associated with particular speech patterns—the Deep South, Scotland, on a seventeenth-century pirate ship, and in a royal court in the Middle Ages. Authors will often write a character's dialogue in what he thinks is a representative dialect. This is far more difficult to do than it would seem. Capturing the style, tone, inflections, and rhythm of a spoken accent with printed words is challenging. The tendency is to overdo the dialect and allow it to become a stereotype, sometimes an offensive stereotype. In writing dialectic dialogue, less is better. The best dialogue lines with local dialect have only a light touch that suggests to the reader what it sounds like. Let the reader create whatever degree of dialect he wants to hear in his imagination. Authors contemplating writing dialect should always keep in mind that in England, the "King's English" used widely at court centuries ago was French.

EDITING DIALOGUE

Your manuscript is complete. Congratulations! Now put it aside for at least two weeks—a month is better. Bury it deep in a drawer. Forget about it. Go on to another project. Resist the temptation to fire off that query letter to agents and editors as soon as possible. Don't do it. If nothing else the agents and editors on your list will thank you.

After a suitable hibernation period, dig the manuscript out of its hiding place and edit it with a fresh perspective. Read the manuscript from front to back, preferably in one sitting, as if you've never seen it before, paying particular attention to the dialogue. Set in your mind that not only have you never seen this novel before, but that also it was written by someone you don't like and that you'd love to find as many problems in the manuscript as possible. Savage it! Tear it apart! Question everything! Gleefully keep a running score of issues by category on a chalkboard. At "The End," set the manuscript down, step back, take a deep breath, and face the fact that you actually wrote this thing. Then warm up the word processor in preparation for some hard, painful editing.

Read the Novel Aloud

Many times authors are advised to read the novel aloud to hear how the dialogue "sounds." Unless the work is a screenplay or children's book, this is not good advice for two reasons. First, when the author reads his own work, he knows the entire story and will use appropriate tone of voice and inflections to make the dialogue sound as he intended, even if it isn't written that way. Second, it's a novel and it's not going to be read aloud. The dialogue has to sound good to someone who has never seen it before and is silently reading the character's words.

A better suggestion is to have someone else who knows nothing about the novel read it to you. Now how does it sound? Next have the same person read to you in a flat, emotionless monotone. Are the meanings and visual images you wanted being carried from the text on the backs of the character's words or not?

Get Critiques

How thick is your skin? Answer: the thicker, the better. Don't give your novel to family members and ask them to critique it. There is almost nothing to be gained, because good or bad they will comment to save your ego and keep peace in the family. Taking a college class will not be particularly helpful either, since faculty tend to have a "look for the silver lining" attitude and look only for good points in the work. A local writers group is sometimes the best place to find someone who will honestly critique your writing. Many writers groups, but not all, have members who are sufficiently comfortable and confident in their writing, and they can give you unvarnished evaluations of your work. If you can accept a harsh critique as a writing professional and deflect the feeling that you are being personally attacked, your writing will show significant improvements.

Reduce the Word Count

As part of the final editing process, authors should squeeze their text, eliminating as many words as possible while still maintaining the meaning. Young adult literature has to be fast-moving. The fewer words to be read, the faster the story moves. I often cringe when an author sends me a query that announces 120,000 or more words in her novel. Unless it's fantasy, this length is difficult to sell. Edit to the absolute minimum number of words required—no more. If it doesn't hurt to cut a word, phrase, sentence, or whole paragraph, it wasn't needed.

Emperor Joseph II, after attending the first performance of The Marriage of Figaro, made the now-famous remark to Mozart, "Too many notes, my dear Mozart." Although the opera would become one of the great classical music works, by the current standard Mozart overornamented it with too many flourishes. The same applies to young adult fiction. "Too many words, my dear author."

Create and Use an Editing Hit List

Writers are creatures of habit, beginning writers more so than experienced ones. As you identify grammar structures, dialogue forms, pet words, qualifiers, and other flaws in your writing, put them on an editing hit list. As you edit a manuscript, use your word processor's find-and-replace (a.k.a. search-and-destroy) function to locate them in the text and correct them. Once identified, you can learn to change your draft writing to avoid them.

SUMMARY

You may have a favorite way to write dialogue. However, there are a lot of potential pitfalls, and good writers don't allow themselves to fall into lazy habits. So here are some excuse-busters to challenge your thinking and dig yourself out of any ruts you may have fallen into.

Everybody Else Does It

"But," an author will say, pointing at a page in another writer's novel, "[popular novelist's name here] does this all the time. Why can't I?" The answer is simple. You are not [popular novelist], and he is. To be taken seriously as a beginning writer with a chance of having your work published, you should be careful when pushing the envelope. Stay with generally accepted standard writing techniques no matter how painfully restricting you might think they are. Trying to lead the train from the caboose in any profession can be difficult. And believe me, I don't say that to limit your creativity.

Read Widely

All writers know that reading the best work in their genres is essential for their own success. Without exception, good writers are good readers. This extends beyond the author's own interests, because there are many crossover novels that fall into two or more genres. Reading a variety of young adult fiction will give you a broader understanding of what is being written and how other authors construct dialogue for scenes and characters that may be wildly different from your own work. A great deal of insight into good technique and the storytelling process can be gained this way.

Keep a log of what novels you have read, and include your observations of why they're good. Record snippets of dialogue, narrative, and scenes that stand out in your mind. Most of all, take notes for yourself of where your efforts fall short of the work of a published author.

Compare Your Work against the Best

Read as many award-winning young adult novels as time permits. EBay and used-paperback bookstores are good sources of inexpensive novels. Compare your work to that of the award-winning authors. At first, this will be a most discouraging process, but put your ego in storage, swallow your pride, and do it anyway. Analyze the differences between your work and theirs—what's good, what's bad, why does this scene in his book work and a similar scene in mine not work? Don't take on the whole novel at once. Pick out a few obvious things that you can improve and fire up the word processor.

Practice, Practice, Practice

So no one wants to look at your first novel and you have a stack of rejections that's so big you're using it for a footstool in your living room? If that's the case, it's time to face the facts. If no one wants your novel, put it away and start the next one. Constantly hawking the same failed book is only taking time away from your writing. Like everything, the more you write, the better your writing becomes. Review what you have been told are your weak points to correct them, focus on your characters and storytelling, and make the next novel better. Repeat this process until an editor or agent does want to look at your work.

CHAPTER 9

FINDING YOUR THEME

The theme of a fable is the moral. The theme of a parable is its teaching. The theme of a novel is much broader because it includes a view of life and how people behave. It's the underlying philosophical idea that the story conveys. In other words, it answers the question, What is the story about?

Your characters have their voices. Your story has its voice. Theme is the writer's voice, your voice, the voice of you caring, your story's soul. Theme is what gets your characters up in the morning. Theme is what keeps your story from sinking.

The theme is critical in a young adult novel, especially one that may be used in school classrooms. At the end of the story, the message of the theme is what the reader takes away. What insights into life or human nature are revealed in the story? How has reading this particular novel affected the reader?

You've already developed your characters and plotted their story, so now let's examine theme. In this chapter you will discover how to find a theme for your novel. You'll determine what it is you want to say to the reader and how to present the message without it taking over the story.

Many writers build a story around a particular theme. These theme-driven stories can be successful. The advantage of this type of story is that the theme is the foundation of the story, and the sooner it's established, the stronger the story will be. The disadvantage is that sometimes choosing a theme first can create a rigid, didactic plot that has a goal of delivering the author's message instead of concentrating on telling an entertaining story. Young adult readers don't want lessons disguised as fiction. They want excitement and characters they can identify with.

However, most writers don't begin with a theme—they have a story to tell, and the theme is part of that story. Too much focus on pinning down a story's theme can limit the emotions and relationships of the characters and their setting, since the author is forcing them into a preconceived mold and not giving them freedom to interact. Most writers find that in the process of telling the story, the theme appears, and the writer can capitalize on it as the story develops.

More than one theme is usually found in a young adult novel. The important central theme grows out of the cause-and-effect relationship between plot events that drive the protagonist toward the climax. It is the general experience or subject that links all the plot details together. Other themes are secondary but still important, since they add detail by dramatizing the characters and enrich the reader's experience with the story.

Let's take a look at a few examples of theme topics. We'll then go through a step-by-step process that will lead you to a theme statement.

PICK A TOPIC

The best themes come as a result of the union of the plot with its conflict, the story, and the interaction of the characters with one another and their settings. Themes should be of universal interest to readers yet focused on the characters of that particular story. If a theme is too simple and too well known, it can come across as cliché.

The following is a list of common theme topics that may be found in a novel.

- Acceptance
- The American Dream
- Artistic talent
- Bringing or coming together
- Challenge and success
- Charity
- Choices and possibilities
- Community and responsibility
- Cooperation
- Courage
- Creative thinking
- Cultural rules of behavior
- Customs and traditions
- Death and how to deal with it
- Development and image of a hero
- Divorce
- Environment
- Family
- Fear
- Forgiveness
- Friendship
- Generosity
- Gratitude
- Growing up or growing old
- Guilt
- Helping
- Honesty
- Honor
- Hospitality
- Human relationships
- Individuality

- Innocence and experience
- Justice
- Keeping a promise
- Kindness
- Knowledge
- Learning
- Liberty and authority
- Listening
- Loneliness
- Love
- Loyalty
- Meaning of freedom
- Mercy
- Nature
- Nonviolence
- Outcast
- Perseverance
- Power and politics
- The power of one
- Priorities
- Racism
- Regret and recovery
- Resistance
- Respect
- Restraint
- Sacrifice
- Science and technology
- Self-awareness
- Selflessness
- Self-esteem
- Sharing
- Tolerance
- War

There are many hundreds of topics, but as they are previously written, none of them are a complete theme, since they are not associated with a particular story and plot. Selecting one of these topics or discovering one or more in a story is the first step toward making a successful theme statement. Let's take a look at a common theme topic in a young adult novel, friendship.

ASK YOURSELF QUESTIONS

By focusing on the theme of friendship the author can ask:

- What started the friendship?
- Did the setting of the story affect the friendship?
- What obstacles stood in the way?
- How were they overcome?
- How was the protagonist affected by the gain or loss of friendship?

Stepping back and examining the topic of friendship running through the story and how it is shaped by the plot, the author can then make a theme statement. In this case it might be: "Friendship is fragile and easily lost, so it must be treated with great care," or "Friendship between kids of different cultural backgrounds requires unusual understanding." At this point the theme statement smoothly fits into the story, and the reader will understand the message at the end of the story.

STATING THE THEME

Once you've picked a topic and have asked yourself a series of questions about the story, you will ultimately be able to create a theme statement. Accurately explaining what a story is about can be difficult for an author. Often this difficulty stems from not having a clear statement of the theme. An author should be able to state the theme of a story in one short declarative sentence. To create a statement of a theme, consider the following.

- **There is no right or set way to determine the theme.** Theme depends on changes to the protagonist and his world, what the protagonist has learned, and the nature of the conflicts and how they were resolved.
- **A theme should be expressed in a complete sentence.** Single words such as "love" or "anger" are not adequate. The statement must present an idea about the topic.
- **The best themes are generalizations about life, society, or human nature.** A theme statement should not refer to a specific character.
- **The theme should not be larger than the details of the story.** While a theme may generalize about an aspect of life, the story is only a small slice of life populated by a limited number of characters. The theme must reflect the realistic limitations of the characters and their settings.
- **Theme is the central unifying concept of a story.** It must account for all of the details in the story, it must not be contradicted by any detail, and it must not rely on supposed facts—facts not actually stated or clearly implied by the story.
- **Any statement that reduces a theme to some familiar saying, aphorism, or cliché should be avoided.** When this happens the theme becomes oversimplified and idealized to the point where actions of the characters are not believable.

The theme is not intended to moralize or teach. In fact, it's not presented directly to the reader at all. It's the nonliteral meaning of a fictional work. The exposition, dialogue, action, and behavior of the characters reflect the theme, and different readers will interpret the meaning of the theme in different ways.

KEY THEME DEVICES

An author should never pronounce what his theme is about inside the story. To be successful the theme must remain invisible and subtly hinted at through other devices in the story and plot. Here are some examples of how you can integrate your theme into your novel without directly coming out and saying it.

- **The protagonist's decision:** The theme should be most visible in the protagonist's greatest choice in the story. What is the protagonist's biggest decision to resolve the story's conflict?

- **Emotions:** The power of emotion in fiction is universal. When an author uses the emotions of the characters to dramatize the theme, the expression of the theme's message becomes unmistakable.

- **Dialogue:** The dialogue of the characters can hint—and no more than hint—at the theme. The danger is that a character, usually the protagonist, will make the theme too obvious through his dialogue. When the author uses his character's voice or narration to state the theme, he is preaching, which will lose most young adult readers.

- **Actions of the protagonist:** The action of the story and the interaction of the protagonist with other characters can function as a mirror held up to the theme, allowing the reader to see it indirectly.

- **Communicating both sides of the theme equally:** Interaction between the protagonist and antagonist can define the theme.

- **Other characters:** The theme can be illustrated by each character representing a different aspect of the theme.

- **Indirect references:** Recurring images, props, colors, settings, and situations can be used to present the theme symbolically in the novel.

THEME EXAMPLES

As examples, the following are statements of themes found in well-known young adult novels. Many of them are taken from the website www.readasummary.com/theme.html.

- There may be other people in the world like us. (*The Borrowers*)
- Some people are just lucky. (*The Boy of the Three-Year Nap*)
- Memories of friendship can last forever. (*Bridge to Terabithia*)
- Defending countries requires loyalty and sacrifices. (*Camp X*)
- Every child is special to his or her family. (*The Canada Geese Quilt*)
- Cats like to be treated kindly. (*Catwings*)
- Kids always want both of their parents. (*Clean Break*)
- Unfortunate children can lead very miserable lives. (*The Convicts*)
- Humor differentiates between humans and animals. (*Dogs Don't Tell Jokes*)
- Imagination can be a powerful weapon. (*Cougar*)
- Jealousy can be destructive. (*The Fairest*)
- Investigation and analysis lead to knowledge. (*From the Mixed-Up Files of Mrs. Basil E. Frankweiler*)
- Feelings make human beings. (*The Giver*)
- Children can face horrific dangers in life. (*Grim Grotto*)
- A human heart can be heavy with secrets. (*The Hatchet*)
- Sometimes we have to accept change even if we don't want to. (*Julie of the Wolves*)
- Some customs and traditions compel people to be dishonest. (*The Kite Runner*)
- Thinking and analyzing contribute to decision making. (*The Lemming Condition*)
- Unity is powerful. (*The Lion, the Witch and the Wardrobe*)
- Some people oppose hunting for fun. (*The Magic Finger*)
- Orphans deserve parental love. (*Molly Moon's Incredible Book of Hypnotism*)
- Children can be brave. (*Molly Moon Stops the World*)

- A sense of belonging is what makes different people stick together. (*The Mountain That Walked*)
- Divorce can lead to miserable children. (*My Broken Family*)
- Families are the basis of life in societies. (*The Orphan of Ellis Island*)
- War has an ugly face that makes children miserable. (*Parvana's Journey*)
- Information leads to knowledge. (*The Penultimate Peril*)
- Sometimes you can save lives by being wise and clever. (*Poppy*)
- Animals care about their homes. (*Poppy's Return*)
- Not everything in life comes without a price. (*Shiloh*)
- Different people can become friends. (*Sign of the Beaver*)
- Sometimes risky decisions yield their fruits. (*Skybreaker*)
- Unfortunate people can sometimes become fortunate. (*The Slippery Slope*)
- Where there is a will, there is a way. (*Stone Fox*)
- Hatred has negative effects on people. (*Weasel*)
- Experiencing misery can help a person understand the real feelings of miserable people. (*The Whipping Boy*)
- Fear can prevent us from helping others. (*Wired*)
- Some people care for wild animals out of sheer love. (*Wolf Pack*)
- Greedy human wolves can be more dangerous than animal wolves. (*The Wolves of Willoughby Chase*)
- Greed makes people cruel animals. (*The Wreckers*)
- Nobody is infallible. (*Harry Potter and the Half-Blood Prince*)
- Believe in miracles. (*The Fire-Eaters*)
- Sometimes ordinary people are capable of extraordinary things. (*The Ropemaker*)
- With perseverance, nothing is out of reach. (*The Land*)
- The abuse of power can lead to destruction. (*The Other Wind*)
- Exploring the mysteries of the past can often unlock answers to the future. (*Briar Rose*)
- By losing everything, sometimes you gain the most precious gift of all: a true sense of self. (*Crispin: The Cross of Lead*)

- Freedom is its own reward. (*The House of the Scorpion*)
- When fate has it in for you, you'd better be prepared. (*Just In Case*)
- Everything has a price, even sacrifice. (*The Astonishing Life of Octavian Nothing, Volume 1*)
- A young girl's understanding of the many rhythms of life, and how she fits within them. (*Heartbeat*)
- Surviving tragedy only makes you stronger. (*Locomotion*)
- One person's actions can have a lifelong impact on another person. (*The River Between Us*)
- When you can't control your own destiny, sometimes it's better to just let fate decide. (*Holes*)
- Even the most breakable hearts in nature can learn to love, to lose, and to love again. (*The Miraculous Journey of Edward Tulane*)
- In the absence of role models, sometimes life's little lessons are best learned on the streets. (*Rules of the Road*)
- Never lose hope, and never stop dreaming. (*True Believer*)
- Only in coming face-to-face with death do we discover the value of living and loving unconditionally. (*Looking for Alaska*)

Plot, theme, and character are all linked. For example, if the cheerleader girlfriend of your main character abruptly breaks up with him and refuses to say why, your theme will probably have something to do with anger and loss. And how your main character acts as he struggles with his feelings about being dumped in this way will deepen his character, move the plot forward, and ultimately connect to the overarching and universal theme of your book or story.

Through plot, we see characters in action; we see how they act and react, think, and feel. For instance, imagine a novel in which the youngest child in a family grows very ill. His older sister puts the needs of their family first and drops out of the high school play she's starring in, in order to help her parents take care of her brother. But the child's older brother—a chess whiz—withdraws into himself and his chessboard; he's so paralyzed by fear that he's unable to help. The plot of the novel is propelled by the illness of the young child and by the reactions and actions of his siblings. The novel will explore the consequences of illness in a family. The overarching and universal theme statement might be that crisis differently affects each person.

In this chapter we've learned how to create a theme statement and have seen how the plot and the characters of your story are the driving force behind it. Try one last exercise, described below, to be sure you are clear on how to create a theme statement.

Our next chapter explores creating the perfect ending. Remember, you do not write the theme statement in your book, not even in the last chapter.

- AUTHOR WORKING -

Author Janice Eidus suggested the following exercise to explore how plot reveals character and links to theme.

Create a scene in which two very different sorts of characters—let's say, a small town's wealthy prom queen and a tough-acting boy from the "wrong side of the tracks"—witness a car accident. The accident propels the plot; now use the characters' actions in this scene to reveal who they are as individuals. Does one of them call for help? Does one try to attend to the needs of the injured? Does one flee from the scene? Does one feel numb and uninvolved? What do their reactions and actions tell us about them? Based upon their responses, what might the next plot action be if this scene were part of a short story or novel? You can set the scene anywhere: a small town, a big city, or a leafy suburb. And instead of a prom queen and a tough kid, perhaps one character can be a loner who spends all her time with computers, and the other can be a budding young poet growing his first mustache and carrying a copy of *On the Road*. And since plot, character, and theme intertwine, perhaps this scene can be leading the reader toward an exploration of the nature of selflessness—or something else, depending upon your world view and vision.

CHAPTER 10

CREATING A SATISFYING CONCLUSION

An ending can be remembered or squandered. You want yours to be remembered.

Endings in young adult fiction are more important to get right than are endings in adult fiction. Many types of endings that may be satisfactory in adult fiction will leave a young adult reader disappointed, unsatisfied, and even angry that the author didn't "finish" the story the way he expected. Authors writing young adult fiction must at all times take into consideration the experience, age, and emotional and psychological development of the reader. (Even though in recent years young adult fiction is being read by adults, too, we must agree that the target readership of young adult fiction ranges from children at the edge of adolescence through almost-adult late teens.) These traits are different from those of adults, and some research into child and adolescent development will help any writer of young adult fiction.

Great young adult novels are more than entertainment. At the end they should have altered the way the reader looks at the world. Ideally, a great young adult novel leaves the reader better able to cope with his own real-world challenges, because he has vicariously lived similar challenges with the protagonist of the story and gained his insights. Like the protagonist, the reader has faced and overcome incredible obstacles and is now stronger and wiser because of his almost-real experiences. As a result, the impression a story leaves on the reader is determined largely by the ending, making the ending doubly important.

Sadly, the ending is where a lot of YA writers seem to lose the proverbial plot. Either the writer tries to resolve everything in the last few pages or else he has too many endings. So my advice to YA writers is to make the ending powerful—think about what will provide the most satisfying ending for your characters. Let it grow out of the situations you've created throughout the book. And, whatever you do, don't send the book out to agents or editors until you have one that really works.

"!!"

- ADVICE FROM PUBLISHERS ROW -

Wendy Lamb, publisher of Wendy Lamb Books:

"The best endings are earned, and by that I mean the emotional payoff the reader feels in that last paragraph is set up early in small moments throughout. You should read that last line and have a true, complete, satisfying understanding of the story. How can so few words do so much work? They can't—their ultimate power depends on preparation.

"Whatever type of book, the author has to prepare the reader for the ending. Build your case for the ending along the way. Subtle moments or details work in a complex, literary book; but a funny wacky book can have a bold *wow* ending. The *wow* will work if the story is already full of such moments."

TYPES OF YOUNG ADULT FICTION ENDINGS

A good ending serves as the keystone of the story, holding up and giving closure to everything that came before. It's the part the author wants the young adult reader to take with him from the story, so it must be well thought out and an integral part of the story. Therefore, the story should end at the moment the theme has been clearly, logically, and entertainingly illustrated for the reader. Not before and never later.

Let's look at some different ending options.

Lessons Learned

The protagonist and possibly other characters recognize that by overcoming the conflict they have learned something important and it will affect their lives.

Open

The author may hint at what the protagonist may do after the climax, but the final interpretation will be left up to the reader. Alternately, the author will leave the protagonist with a number of equally plausible courses of action, and the reader must decide which the character will choose. In this ending the hints and choices must be tightly coupled to the plot and proceed logically from the character.

Cliffhanger

Ending with a cliffhanger can be done, but it must be approached with great care. The major conflict must be completely resolved, and all of the loose ends except one must be resolved. That single remaining loose end must be selected to generate the reader's interest for a sequel and at the same time be significant enough to be used to begin the next novel.

Circular

In this ending the protagonist returns home to tell of his life-changing quest. Often the end scene is similar or the same as the beginning. This ending is frequently used in fantasy novels.

Wish or Promise

The story ends with the protagonist wishing for a different outcome of the climax or making promises to himself that will affect his life. This type of ending is common in young adult fiction, but it can be overdone. The promises must be reasonable extensions from the plot that the character can actually carry out.

Reversal

In a reversal ending a character may start with nothing and end up with everything or begin with nothing and lose it all. What is being gained or lost does not have to be physical objects, such as riches. Love, happiness, friendship, trust, and many other intangible things may be won and lost in the course of a story.

Resolution

The story builds to a climax where the protagonist either "wins" or "loses" in his quest to resolve the conflict. Generally there are clear winners and losers, but the protagonist does not always have to be the winner.

Bittersweet

The protagonist must make a difficult decision and sacrifice something to obtain something else. These endings work well because, as in real life, when a conflict is overcome, there is an element of loss along with the victory. The best bittersweet endings require that the protagonist make a choice among things, all of which are important, and where giving one up will cause him significant pain and remorse.

Puzzle

This ending is a variation on the resolution ending. In this ending a mystery is solved or explained. Usually the reader is enlightened at the same time as the protagonist, but sometimes the protagonist is left in the dark.

Twist

To be successful, this ending must truly surprise the reader, but the surprise must extend logically from the plot of the story. It should not be a coincidence or "just in the nick of time" random event. This type of ending is hard to write well, and if done poorly it will seem like a punch line to an extended joke.

Train Wreck

Unlike many types of endings there is no element of surprise in a train wreck. The protagonist's life or situation spirals down to an inevitable disaster that readers can see coming but the protagonist can't. The plot of a story with this type of ending must be carefully unwound because the reader knows the nature of the climax. How it's presented must follow logically and have its own unique, interest-holding qualities.

Revelation

Revelation uses rising tension in the form of the choices being continually narrowed until a final choice is revealed that explains all.

Monologue

In a monologue ending, the protagonist alone comments about the outcome of the climax. These should be short and written to allow the reader leeway to interpret the character's words. A closing monologue can easily be overdone and turn into a preaching lecture to the reader.

Narrative

The narrator takes over and wraps up the plot by discussing the climax instead of the characters. Narrator endings should be short and to the point, referring to the characters as much as possible. The reader has developed a relationship with the characters and does not want the narrator to take the story over from the protagonist.

Reflection

This is a variation of the narrative ending where the narrator thinks about the climax and muses about the characters' futures. The narrator discusses the climax and plot only indirectly while discussing the protagonist more directly.

Dialogue

Two or more characters discuss the climax and its ramifications. This ending works best when it is kept short. Lengthy summaries of the plot and the climax are counterproductive. The reader should know what has happened and why and does not need the characters to tell him.

Literal Image

In this ending the setting or some aspect of the setting resolves and completes the plot. A common use of this ending is in fantasy novels where the protagonist resolves the conflict by successfully positioning himself in a desired location.

Symbolic Image

Details described in a setting or a situation represent a meaning beyond the literal one. An author should exercise great caution in this type of ending, because the readers may miss the point altogether if the symbolism is beyond their experience and maturity. This is not commonly found in young adult fiction. If symbolism is used, it works better when coupled together with another, more concrete type of ending.

Illuminating

At first read, this type of ending seems abrupt because it does not have a traditional clear-cut resolution. However, the ending does indicate what will happen to the characters, implying that now that the conflict has been overcome, life will go on as it was before. This type of ending is rarely used in young adult fiction.

Epilogue

This type of ending is not normally found in young adult fiction. If used, it tends to be a summary of the future life of the protagonist and should relate to the consequence of the story. It should be exceedingly brief, because it can tell the readers what would be better left to their imaginations.

TEN ENDINGS TO AVOID AT ALL COSTS

There are some endings that really just get under your skin. Granted, these radioactive do-not-touch endings are still being used, sometimes with great success, but such instances are extremely rare, and unless an author has a variation that is unique, exciting, and fresh, he should avoid them. Let's consider a few and why they aren't the most effective.

And Then I Woke Up

This ending is the author bailing out on the reader. After writing many pages of an interesting, exciting story, the author has run out of energy or imagination. The "waking to a ringing alarm clock" ending is an example of this.

And Then I Died

An ending such as this is a bailout by the author similar to the ending above. This ending has been overwritten so many times that it's a cliché unworthy of a good story.

I Found Out That I'd Been Dead All Along

The "speaking from the grave" ending is old and stretches the readers' willingness to suspend their logic to enjoy the story. There is a limit as to how much a reader is willing to accept, and this exceeds it.

And Their Names Were Adam and Eve

If a story ends with a population-destroying holocaust or a couple who have crash-landed on an environmentally suitable planet, don't try to end with this gambit. No one will believe it.

The Vengeance Ending

With this ending the downtrodden protagonist extracts his vengeance on the antagonist, regaining his dignity and honor. The nerd on the beach takes the Charles Atlas muscle course to become more than a match for the sand-kicking bully. A vengeance ending can be effective only if it is consistent with the personality of the character that has been fashioned throughout the novel. The reader has had an entire novel to assess and understand the protagonist's motivations. A revenge ending would have to have been developed and foreshadowed long before the climax, and it would follow logically from the personality and motivations of the character. One of the best examples of a revenge ending in any fictional work is the ending of the movie *The Sting*. At the climax, the grifters get revenge on the big-time hood so subtly that the victim didn't know he'd been played as a sucker even as he lost all his money. Most important, the grifters each played roles faithful to their abilities and personalities established from the beginning of the film and took advantage of the antagonist's weakness. In a vengeance ending the author has to decide if his character has the personality and motivation to spend the time and effort to challenge his antagonist's strong point as the nerd on the beach would do, or exploit some weakness or flaw in his enemy.

And the Next Day in the Paper I Saw That He Died

This is the "I talked to a ghost and didn't know it" ending. For some unknown reason, spirits wander the night doing good deeds for people. A common variation is the "I picked up a ghost hitchhiker." This ending fails because it introduces a new character at the end, a character so important that a short appearance at or near the climax can alter the course of the entire novel. Instead of resolving all the conflicts and bringing the novel to a close, the author has created a host of unanswered questions with a new character. The reader will want to know who this spirit is and what relationship it has to the protagonist that makes him so important. In short, the novel really doesn't end.

And It Was the Man in a Mask All the Time

This ending often surfaces in ghost and horror stories where the supernatural being is really a person in disguise. Fiction requires the reader to suspend belief and allow his imagination to accept the premise of the story as reality. In this story the reader wants to believe in the supernatural entity. But posing a human character as a supernatural being so effectively that the protagonist can't see through the disguise for the entire novel will disappoint the reader and chop off the peak of the tension. A story should maintain the internal logic the author has written into the plot from the beginning. The climax should be the inevitable last sequence of scenes leading up to it. Changing the entire nature of the supernatural being is akin to climbing a flight of stairs and missing the last step, so the reader's expectations are never fully realized.

And It Was My Evil Twin; We Were Separated at Birth

With this ending, the reader finds that the tension about who the evil character in the novel is is really just a case of mistaken identity. A variation of this is the stable boy who discovers he is really the lost son of a rich family or royalty who was somehow separated from his family at birth. This ending violates the trust the reader has put in the author to tell a consistent story. By the climax, what the protagonist has to gain or lose must be important enough so that the reader can sympathize with the character's situation and vicariously participate in it. The reader wants to experience the same emotions as the protagonist. Arriving at the climax and discovering that it was all a mistake or misunderstanding defuses the tension of the climax and makes the protagonist's quest an exercise in futility, letting down the reader.

Really I'm a Dog/Cat/Alien/Demon/Angel

If the reader thinks for the entire novel that the protagonist is one creature only to find that he is something altogether different, he will feel cheated. When a reader cares about a character, he is not going to like having that character weirdly transformed at the end of the story. The climax should be foreshadowed throughout the novel, leading up to the climax, and each scene should support and anticipate the next. If at the last minute the plot cuts away from the logical progress of the story to drop a contrived surprise twist on the reader, the reader's imagination will be jarred and he will no longer believe the reality of the world created from the beginning of the novel.

Pun or Play on Words

The entire story is a setup for a putrid pun or a banal play on words at the end. This is most often seen in short stories, but occasionally it will show up in a novel—a trick guaranteed to anger a reader.

***

If a writer closely analyzes these endings, it can be seen that they all fail for the same reason. After reading tens of thousands of words, the reader is involved and committed to the story. He knows the characters and cares about them, he knows the setting, and he knows the relationships that drive the interactions between the characters. In other words, he has expectations of what the ending will be based on everything the author has given him since the beginning. When the author uses one of the above endings, he derails the reader's anticipation of the end and creates a huge intellectual pile-up of disappointment. The author has not delivered on the promise he made to the reader at the beginning of the story. From the artistic point of view of the story, such endings are dishonest. If an author has invested time to create a compelling story for the reader, surely by the end of the story the creative well has not yet run so dry that the author can't create an equally compelling ending.

A general rule is that if you've heard it or seen it before, especially in a popular movie, television program, or bestselling story, it's probably already overused and you should think twice before including it.

HOW TO END A YOUNG ADULT NOVEL RIGHT

When he writes that first line, an author makes a bargain with the reader. In return for readers buying and reading the author's book, the author promises that the story will be emotionally and intellectually satisfying. To be successful an author must make good on this promise, because the reader will forget the beginning and remember the ending and will evaluate the work on that memory.

How does an author end a young adult novel so that the reader is satisfied and is looking for other stories by the same writer? First of all, consider that the ending consists of the entire final scene of the story, which is often a number of pages. The ending is made up of the last events and character interactions that close the story. It usually, but not always, wraps up the resolution of the conflict and ties up any loose ends. Sometimes parts of the conflict and certain obstacles remain open but are intensified to dramatize the final decisions made by the protagonist. If something is left unresolved, the ending should provide the reader with a sense of how it might be resolved in the future. Whatever strategy the author uses, it must follow logically with the plot, theme, and tone of the story.

The precursors of a satisfying ending are found at the beginning of the story. Somewhere near the first few pages of plot, an incitement event takes place. This event causes a chain of other events to occur that will eventually lead to the climax and the ending. These events are linked with cause-and-effect relationships, and one event follows logically from the next as the protagonist and other characters react to each situation. At the end, the reader must be able to look back along the length of the chain of events of the plot, see the beginning, and say, "Oh, I get it." On the other hand, the author should be able to look down the chain from the beginning and see the ending as the last link that effectively ends the story. Many authors write the ending of the story right after the beginning and then fill in the middle. In this way both ends of the chain of cause and effect in the plot can be seen and are firmly anchored.

A formula for a satisfying ending for a story has four parts, although all four may or may not be used in a particular novel, depending on the plot.

1. An Echo of the Plot, Conflict, and Theme

At the end, the reader should be able to look back and see the chain of events that placed the protagonist in his current position. The reader should understand how the protagonist got there and, more important, why he's there. The events of the plot, the theme, and the resolution of the plot should all add up to the message that a reader will take away from the experience of reading the novel.

2. A Display of the Character's Feelings

In young adult fiction a change is brought upon the protagonist. He has been through great challenges, and the reader must believe that what has transpired has significance. The reader is sympathetic to the main character and wants to see the effects of overcoming the conflict in the behavior of the character—if only briefly. Deep emotions colored and shaped by the conflict should be on full display at the end.

3. The Impact of the Decision Made by the Protagonist to Resolve the Conflict

To have a good story the outcome of the conflict must be important to the protagonist. In the same way, the decision made by the character must reflect this importance so that when the decision is made it will have a powerful effect. Young adult fiction should reflect real-life choices made by the readers. Seldom do we get exactly what we want. Often, young adult readers must choose among alternatives, all of which may be desirable. They want to see those choices reflected in the books they read.

4. The Future

Given that the protagonist has made a difficult choice, how will he fare in the future? In the final lines an author may wish to hint at possible other conflicts or satisfying scenarios that the character may experience. Some authors add an epilogue to give the reader a peek ahead, but these are not particularly well received by readers who would rather use their own imaginations to plan the character's future.

HINTS FOR STORY ENDINGS

The following are some suggestions that can be used to design a satisfying ending.

Make Sure the Ending Fits the Story

Successful endings often have multiple layers with more than one thing going on at the same time. In this way, no single character or action has to carry the entire load of wrapping up the story. Throughout the novel, the protagonist shares the experience with other characters in different scenes. The ending should be shared as well.

Be True to Your Characters

If the characters have shown their personalities in a particular way all through the story so far, don't make a dramatic change as a device to end the story. The reader should have great sympathy for them by now; don't take that away by creating a new character's personality in the old character's body.

Leave a Teaser

Now that the characters have completed the story, there's nothing wrong with leaving some uncertainty as to what the future will bring, as long as the main conflict has been wrapped up.

Pace the Ending Like the Plot

If the plot has moved along a brisk pace through the story, don't drag the reader down into a leisurely, lengthy narration or conversation at the end. Keep it moving.

Don't Add New Information

Avoid introducing new information, characters, objects, scenes, and so on. The story is wrapping up, and everything the reader needs to know to close the story should be on display by now.

Avoid the Trite

The conflict is exceedingly important to the protagonist. For the entire length of the story, the author has tried to link the reader's emotions to those of the characters in the unfolding plot. When the ending is trite or banal, the reader will be disappointed and dismissive of the theme and message.

Don't Moralize

Although young adult fiction often has a message for the reader, the ending of the story should be as empty of the direct personality and opinions of the author as possible. The end should be the final demonstration of the theme and the end of the story, pointedly carried by the characters in the final message scene, not in the narrator's or protagonist's voice.

Don't Be Melodramatic

The climax and ending should have the maximum impact on the reader, but avoid melodrama. The tone of the end should follow directly from the tone of the story. Unnecessarily ramping up the emotional content to heighten the impact will be easily recognized as faux tension. There is a fine line between maximum impact and fatal impact, and crossing it will turn the reader off.

Don't Overwrite

Through the editing process, an author may keep adding more and more layers to the ending scene. This isn't necessary if the story has been told well. Trust the readers: they'll understand and remember the meaning without having it told to them again.

Don't Prolong the Ending, but Don't Abbreviate It Either

Give the ending as much space as it needs to get the job done, but not too much. Not every detail has to be discussed, nor should the plot be summarized. Take into consideration what the reader knows from the story and build on it to bring it to closure.

CHAPTER 11

GETTING CONSTRUCTIVE FEEDBACK

For months you've been working on your manuscript. You've weathered writer's block for several weeks and made it through to the end. In a blaze of excitement you are raring to start sending it to agents. *Stop.* I can't tell you how many times I've been sent the first draft of a manuscript. (How can I tell? Because it's riddled with typos, errors, and inconsistencies.) You've spent so much time working through all the elements of the work; please don't allow your manuscript to get passed on because of silly mistakes that could have been avoided.

Let me give you an example. I was watching the latest DVD version of a TV show I like. One episode revealed that the main character's father had abandoned him as a baby. Afterward, I went back and watched the entire show from beginning to end. In season one, this same character mentioned a clear memory of growing up with both his mother and father. Obviously the show's writers didn't catch this small change of premise; I might not have caught it had I not been watching all the DVDs back to back. But this small story illustrates exactly why you should carefully read and revise your manuscript after it's finished—to look for all those little details that need polishing, revising, moving, or cutting. This chapter includes information on rewriting, seeking advice from fellow writers, and developing community through critique groups. It will also cover information on how to get the most out of your participation in writers conferences.

REVISIONS

It may have taken you several months, if not years, to finish your manuscript, and of course you feel like all along the way you have been self-checking for all the pertinent craft elements that we spoke of in earlier chapters. You may have even told yourself, "I've done my revisions already on a chapter-by-chapter basis." If that's true— excellent. But I urge you to go through the revision process even so; you never know what you may find to improve your manuscript.

Prepare yourself to do a series of revisions. You'll be the first to revise your manuscript, but you'll also revise based on feedback from a critique group or writing buddy, your agent, and your editor. The revision process can be very daunting and quite an emotional experience.

There are many ways to go about revising your work. I've found that the following process eliminates a lot of the editorial requests for revision that you might otherwise get.

1. **Give yourself a little distance from the manuscript.** If you have time to put it down for a week or two, great. This will allow you to come back to it with fresh eyes. You should ask yourself: Why did I write this story? And why should someone read it? Does it really have a core reason to exist?

2. **Read the manuscript aloud.** Often reading aloud will help you feel the pace. If there's too much description, you will find yourself getting fatigued by it. If there's too much dialogue or you have too many characters, you might find yourself getting lost in it.

3. **Reread the manuscript in one sitting if possible.** Make notes in places that you might need to come back to and look at again, but don't make corrections at this point.

4. **Go back to your notes.** Fix those things that instantly popped out at you.

5. **Before you arbitrarily start chopping up your manuscript, ask yourself a few overall questions.**

   a. *Content:* Does the story have narrative drive, emotional power, and an original style?

   b. *Character:* Are the characters believable?

   c. *Voice:* Does the dialogue sound authentic?

   d. *Execution:* Does the story have sufficient pace and appeal or literary value?

   e. *Quality of Writing:* Does the story have adequate balance of dialogue, description, and action?

   f. *Age Appropriateness:* Is the content age-appropriate in language and message?

7. **Start trimming.** There's usually material that can be cut or shortened. Look for inconsistencies, poor transitions, and words repeated too often.

8. **Read the first page.** Agents and editors pay very close attention to the first couple of pages of your manuscript. Make sure those pages really draw the reader in. Is there something unique about the character or the setup that will make the reader want to continue?

9. **Do a grammar and punctuation revision.** Don't get distracted by this too early—it should be the last thing you do. There's plenty of time to catch these errors later.

As you are revising, don't worry about how long it will take you to tighten the manuscript. Editors and agents would prefer to see a well-polished manuscript than one that was rushed to their desk, especially after feedback has been provided. Michelle

Poploff, vice president and editorial director at Delacorte, says, "I have an open conversational style with my authors. They know they can send me an email asking any questions about the process at any time. We communicate through emails, comments on the manuscript, meet in person when possible, or set up a mutually convenient time for extended telephone conversations. We go back and forth with ideas, suggestions, comments, and so on, for as long as it takes."

I love revising and tweaking. (In fact, I'm sure my editor for this book at several points had wished I would just hurry up already.) Understandably, though, not everyone likes revising. But there are a few things to remember about this process.

First, everyone gets edited. I have never—and I do mean never—had a client whose manuscript came in perfect and didn't get some editorial feedback. So don't think you're being singled out.

Also, when you've been offered editorial advice from someone in your critique group or even from your editor, you don't have to take the advice. I say this sheepishly because I don't want to send the wrong message. To be clear: when given editorial advice you don't have to necessarily take the suggestion, but you must fix the problem. Author Bethany Hegedeus says, "Working with your editor is like working with a therapist. They help you articulate the vision of what you want and work to guide you, but you still have to do all the work." I always tell my authors that they must stay true to the vision of their work; be authentic but be flexible. Editors have reasons for making their suggestions, and unless you feel very strongly about it, and sometimes you will, do take the suggestion. If you plan to stick to your idea, you must be able to justify it. And as you are formulating your justification for leaving it, be sure to think of your reader first.

Often you'll need some time to think about how to make the changes. Be sure that when you make revisions you keep all the varying versions. I always date the file of my manuscripts, and I keep each version so that I can go back to the files later. You'll find that sometimes things you've cut in one round may creep back into your manuscript later, or possibly into a future book.

You don't have to feel like you are on your own when it comes to revising. There are many ways to get the feedback you need before sending your manuscript out to agents. The remaining sections will give you some examples of how to get others to review your novel.

"!!"

- ADVICE FROM PUBLISHERS ROW -

Stacey Barney, editor at Penguin Putnam:

"Writers are the bravest people in the world and are defined not by publishing credits but by their courage and willingness to follow their muse despite even the most withering of critiques, their commitment to their craft, and their generosity of spirit. It's a brave and generous thing to share words, stories, characters as personal to the creator as their most guarded secrets. Writers, from the novice and unknown to the most accomplished, are the heart, conscious conscience, and soul of humanity—the best of who we are and our mirror. I thank God for writers every day."

CRITIQUE GROUPS

While some writers are eager to release their work and send it to editors right off, others are a bit more hesitant. You hesitate to send it out, then you go ahead and release it and wish you hadn't. If you do this, a critique group can make that process easier.

- AUTHOR WORKING -

Author Sundee Frazier says, "To me, writing a novel without seeking the input of trusted readers would be like trying to swim the English Channel alone. You're just asking for trouble. The best input confirms something you already suspected but were too scared or proud or lazy to change. There's also the inevitability that others will see meaning and connections in your work that you didn't even realize you were creating. This kind of feedback goes a long way toward motivating me to complete my manuscript (or getting me to the other side of the channel, if you will). My first novel for young people would not have been nearly as good or complete if it weren't for the suggestions of others. The entire tone of the book, where it starts, the cast of characters, and even the accessibility of the main character would have been much different had it not been for the constructive commentary of those to whom I entrusted my work."

When setting up your own critique group, be sure to provide the readers with a list of overall questions so that they can evaluate your work. It's best when you have all readers review based on a consistent set of parameters. That way you can determine if there's uniformity in the remarks. In addition to the questions you asked yourself earlier, you may want to ask some or all of the following questions.

- Does the title reflect the content of the book?
- Does the first page grab your attention?
- Does the first chapter engage the reader and set up the basis for the rest of the story?

- Do you care about the characters?
- Have I provided enough emotional content to involve the reader?
- Is the basic premise or theme interesting?
- Is it believable?
- Is it unique?
- Is the point of the novel presented clearly, and is it apparent to the reader?
- Are general facts and information accurate and consistent throughout?
- Is the language level (e.g., word choice, syntax, sentence structure) appropriate for the genre and consistent throughout?
- Is the basic premise of the novel appealing and well executed?

If you plan to set up your own critique group and you don't know anyone offhand, you should definitely hit the blogosphere. There are hundreds of blogs that speak directly to the young adult market. One of the most comprehensive I've found is www.asuen. com/blog.central.kid.lit.html. It is run by Anastasia Suen, author of more than one hundred books. Blogs are not only a way to get feedback on your novel prepublication but also a way to develop community around your book so that you can gain a readership. Once you have developed a community, they will support you once the book is published. Readers who gave feedback feel part ownership in its development. In addition, creating one's own blog has become so commonplace in the young adult market it is almost a means of entry into the community of readers.

Oftentimes authors will post a chapter on their Facebook page and solicit responses or get feedback. This is another option. In fact, the Internet is full of social networking sites—websites designed to introduce people to other people—that can be used to your advantage. Sites like Facebook and MySpace allow you to create a web page dedicated to your work. You can also join groups of other potential YA authors where you can solicit feedback. Turn the Web to your advantage—use it to publicize and polish your work.

CONFERENCES

An additional option for getting feedback on your manuscript is to participate in writers conferences. As the number of aspiring authors has increased over the last decade, so has the number of conferences all around the world. There are conferences for nearly every genre of book, including young adult books. A writers conference can be a treasure trove of information.

At the average conference you'll find workshops, keynote speakers, round-table discussions, moderated group sessions, writing exercises focusing on the craft of writing, one-on-one consultations with industry experts, and critique sessions. There are also personalized writing retreats for individuals and group writing retreats.

To find out more and to review a list of conferences, there's an online resource called ShawGuides that features conferences and writers' retreats around the world. It can be found at writing .shawguides.com.

The registration fee for the average conference can start as low as $100, but it's usually more on the average of $500, depending on the location, the cast of professionals in attendance, and the history of successful writers who may have gotten their start there.

In assessing what conference to attend, be sure to find out if you will have the opportunity to have one-on-one consultations with editors or agents. This is invaluable even if your manuscript is still in the early stages. They can provide you with feedback early on, and sometimes that feedback may even take your manuscript in a totally different direction. Not only is the feedback helpful, but it also sets the stage for the opportunity to submit your work to the editor or agent later once you've finished.

When you have a one-on-one consultation with an editor or agent you may be asked to pitch your project to them in a very short time period. Some conferences pattern it after speed dating, where you only get five minutes to tell the editor or agent about your work. This forces you to have a succinct and clear message about your book, similar to what you might see on the back cover. But you also have to tell the editor or agent a bit about you as an author. It can be very nerve-racking, and it takes some skill to pull it off. However, editors and agents know how difficult this is, so often they will have a workshop set up for writers who plan to pitch, where they teach you all about how to do it. There are even books about it. One of my dear friends, Katharine Sands, has a book called *Making the Perfect Pitch*. It has helped many a writer with not only pitching at conferences but also writing the perfect query letter.

I always find it interesting when I'm at conferences and people sit down to pitch their story ideas to me. It's not always the best pitches that produce the best books. However, those who can pitch their projects with aplomb are the ones I initially get excited about. Unfortunately, a writer's personality, character, and dramatic effect are not always the same as what is found in the manuscript. The author's style is often what sets her apart in this media-driven marketplace. If you can get someone excited by you and your personality, they will often take a second look.

There are typically a number of agents at the conference, and you will need to size them up quickly to determine who you will want to pitch your project to. The conference organizers will ask participants to sign up for one-on-one meetings. The list can fill up quickly. If you are not able to get a one-on-one because you didn't sign up fast enough, there may be other opportunities to speak to your ideal agent or editor during the conference.

Agents and editors will speak on panels describing the kind of books they are interested in. You might have an opportunity to tell them a little about your project after the panel discussion. As

much as you may be tempted, don't pitch your work during the
Q&A session of the panel. Another place you may be able to get
specific feedback on your project is during a workshop session.
Agents will sometimes ask for volunteers to share their work or
use it as an example during their course. Not only will you get
advice on your work but they may also request to see the full
manuscript later.

The conference is also a place to meet other writers and form
relationships. There are often critique groups being formed.

YOUNG ADULT WRITING PROGRAMS

While this book was written to help teach you to write for the
young adult market, you can educate yourself beyond these pages.
There are a number of programs to help writers develop their
writing skills for the YA market. I've found that most of the writers
who have participated in these programs have landed at least an
agent, and many go on to publish their work as well. Both agents
and editors troll these programs for great talent.

And the exciting thing about several of them is that you don't
have to leave your home to participate. Vermont College, which
designed the first ever MFA program for children's and young adult
literature, has a low-residency model that allows students to work
directly with faculty through written correspondence, online work,
and telephone conference calls. Other similar programs include
Seton Hall, Lesley College, the New School, Rutgers, and Stanford
University. I've included additional information on these programs
in the appendix.

THE PROFESSIONAL EDITOR

Finally, there's one other way to get feedback on your writing—
you can pay for it. (I mention this process last because it is the most
expensive way to do it.) You can hire a professional literary coach,

book doctor, or editor. The good thing about it is that if you hire someone good, your manuscript will be extremely polished. The bad thing is that the cost can be somewhat prohibitive depending on the professional.

If you are interested in going this route, you can ask editors, agents, published authors, or writing friends for referrals. Ideally you want to find someone who focuses his editorial development work on YA books. There are some companies that do just that—for example, namelos.com, run by former Front Street Books president Stephen Roxburgh. You can also go to publishersmarketplace .com. This website is chock-full of editors who can help you develop your work. Again, be sure the editor you choose is one who works on YA books, because he will be most knowledgeable about what agents want to see and the sensibilities of the market. And of course there are directories, such as *The National Directory of Editors and Writers for Hire*, compiled by Elizabeth Lyon, as well as publishersmarketplace.com

CHAPTER 12

FINDING AN AGENT

There comes a time when you're ready to take your material to the public. This chapter will show you how to write query letters, contact agents, and determine which agents are best for your career.

THE AGENT'S ROLE

After you've written your manuscript, revised it, had it critiqued, and then revised it again, you're ready to send it out to agents.

Now, you may be thinking at this point, "I don't need an agent. I have a friend who got published without an agent, and I'm sure my manuscript is just as good if not better than hers. I know someone will love it." Or you might be thinking, "Well, when I went to the conference, I met an editor who told me to send it directly to her once I finished it. I really don't think I'll try to find an agent until after someone has taken me on." Or you might be thinking, "Well, it's just as hard to find an agent as it is to find an editor, so I might as well just skip the agent step."

I've heard all these theories and more from novice writers. I'll just say this: the industry has become exceedingly more complicated over the last twenty years, and agents do a lot more than just sell the manuscript. Let's take a closer look at all the different things today's agents do and why it is to your benefit to have an agent.

Most of the major publishing houses today take very few, if any, unsolicited manuscripts. That means if you haven't been asked to submit your materials, they will be sent back to you or may sit in a slush pile until an assistant picks them up (if anyone ever does).

Many say that securing an agent is just as difficult as finding an editor. I'm here to tell you that that can often be true. However, there is a reason for this. Agents and editors think alike. You'll find that many agents were editors before they became agents. Agents are keenly aware of a great story and what it will take to sell it to an editor and to the marketplace. Because of this, editors trust agents. If you are able to secure an agent, you'll have a much better chance of getting your work published than a writer who doesn't have an agent.

What Agents Do

- Act as a business representative
- Negotiate rights and collect funds on behalf of the author
- Review clients' work and offer advice on its quality and potential marketability
- Give advice on current trends, practices, and contract terms
- Offer editorial advice
- Selectively submit your work to appropriate editors
- Sell subrights (movie options, merchandising, ebook rights)

"!!"

- ADVICE FROM PUBLISHERS ROW -

Steven Malk, Writers House:

Steven encourages writers to slow down and take their time with the process.

"It's a big decision that you should take very seriously. Your goal should be to make as educated, thoughtful, and careful of a decision as possible. You want to have a very long career, so in the grand scheme of things, taking an extra six or even twelve months to do your research, understand the marketplace, and find the best fit for you isn't a big deal." Steven is interested in taking on clients who understand the business. "Don't come across as an author who is dabbling, but rather as someone who is very serious and committed to this business."

Rachel Coyne, Fine Print Literary Management:

Rachel points to three things she looks for in authors:

1. Authors who write to evergreen genres and/or themes—genres that seem to thrive year after year.

2. Authors who are flexible and don't mind making editorial changes.

3. Authors who come to the table in a professional manner and are able to understand the business side of publishing, and authors who respect that the book is a product.

Understanding Agents

One thing that complicates this business quite a bit is that it's very fluid. Historically, authors would establish a relationship with an editor, and they would pretty much work with that editor for most if not all of their career. That is no longer the case. Editors move from one publishing house to another quite frequently. So now the anchor relationship is the author-agent relationship. Agents spend a lot of their time building relationships. Most agents will take at least one or two meetings a week trying to establish relationships with editors. If an editor moves, the agent has to stay current on the types of books the editor might be looking for. While an editor's taste typically doesn't change, the needs of a given house might. So one publishing house may publish mostly YA, and then the new house publishes mostly picture books. It's difficult if you aren't following the business closely to stay current with the numerous moves.

Understanding agents and their jobs is important to working well with them. There are a number of things that agents have in common.

- **Numerous submissions:** I typically receive at least seventy-five queries or submissions a week. That's quite a bit of reading, to say the least.
- **Financial pressure:** Agents are paid a 15 percent commission on the work they sell. It's not until they sell a manuscript that they get compensated. All the reading they do is done for free. As a result, this is one of the reasons that agents send form rejection letters—again, limited time. Their time must be spent on selling books that they believe in.
- **Shifting priorities:** At any given time an agent may be reading manuscripts, giving editorial advice, having lunch with an editor, negotiating a contract, responding to editorial questions, participating in workshops or conferences, or a host of other tasks.
- **Limited time:** Agents are responsible for so many varying aspects of the business, and as such, they are always trying to balance their time. You should not become frustrated if you don't hear back immediately on a submission.

What Agents Don't Do

- **Offer tax or general legal advice.** While agents are intimately familiar with publishing agreements and are more than capable of negotiating them on your behalf, that's pretty much where it ends. They are not attorneys, and when things go beyond the agreement they often suggest you hire legal consultation. The same goes for accounting advice.

- **Act as a publicist for the author's books.** For those who are new to the industry, the role of the publicist and the role of the agent can be somewhat confusing. Publicists help you get your book in front of media—that includes online, print, radio, and television. And while agents are always supportive of this role, they don't take on this role as a part of their responsibility.

HOW TO FIND AN AGENT

How do you go about securing an agent? There are a number of guides both in print and online where you can review agents and the kind of clients they represent. You can check with the Association of Authors' Representatives (www.aaronline.org); *The Guide to Literary Agents*, published annually by Writer's Digest Books; or *Jeff Herman's Guide to Book Publishers, Editors, and Literary Agents*, among others. This is also an opportunity to go back to the critique group that you established. One of the best ways to get an agent to look at your work is to have someone refer you. I always look at authors who are referred to me first.

Before you start to approach an agent, here's a list of questions you should be able to answer first.

- **Will I write both young adult books and adult books during my career?** Some agents handle only children's and YA, and if you know that you might have an adult book in your future you may want to work with an agent that handles both adult and YA.

- **Will I need assistance with promoting my work once it's published?** Some agents, while they are not publicists, spend time strategizing with the author on how to get his book out into the public.

- **Do I need an agent who has strong editorial skills as well as selling skills?** While many agents come from editorial backgrounds, some come from sales, from law, or from other fields totally removed from the editorial process. If that's the case, they might not be able to dig in and provide a lot of editorial development guidance. That may be okay for you if you are handling that part on your end by working with critique groups or a professional editor.

- **Will I want to be able to meet my agent in person?** Because so many agents are based in the New York tri-state area, many have not met clients they have worked with for years who live in another part of the country. The relationship is established and maintained via phone and email. Some writers may want a more in-person relationship with their agent, so location may be important.

Researching Agencies

If this is your first time trying to get your work published and you are not familiar with literary agents, please pay close attention to this section. There are numerous literary agents in the business. They are not all created equal.

You should first research the agent's credentials. You will want to have a sense of how long the agent has been in business. There are advantages and disadvantages to working with new or seasoned agents. Often new agents are hungrier and will work harder to develop you, but they may not have as many connections. Seasoned agents may not have as much time for you and often are more difficult to approach because they take on so few new clients.

NOTE: There are agents out there who are called "for fee" agents. You should not work with these agents. They charge you for reading your manuscript, critiquing, and editorial guidance. Reputable agents consider this practice unethical.

Here's a checklist of elements you can use as a basis for comparing agents. Think about each aspect and which elements are most important to you.

- ☐ How long in the business
- ☐ Location
- ☐ Referrals
- ☐ Commission structure
- ☐ Size of agency
- ☐ Number of clients
- ☐ Agent history
- ☐ Terms of representation
- ☐ Contacting agents

Once you've figured out the agent you plan to approach, you will need to prepare a query letter. There will likely be multiple agents who meet your criteria. It is okay and also advisable that you approach numerous agents. Most agents specify through their submission guidelines how they wish to be contacted—i.e., snail mail or electronically. But they all require a query letter. So let's take a look at how to write one.

Query Letters

A query letter is the first piece of writing that your agent will see. If done well, it becomes the golden ticket and will open the door to your sending your full manuscript.

Your query letter should be just as stylized as your book itself. It should broadcast to your agent the brilliance of the manuscript to come.

The agent will use this query as a basis for writing her own submission letter, and editors may use it later to create tip sheets, back cover copy, or other means to promote the book. So spend some time honing it. It's your entrée to the world of publishing.

I should warn you that most agents nowadays prefer electronic submissions. However, if you decide to send a snail mail copy as follow-up to an online submission, here are some overall dos and don'ts for the query letter:

- Never send more than a one-page letter. Prove that you can write concisely.
- Use white or ivory paper.
- Use twelve-point font, single line space, and black ink.
- Do not use fancy script; keep it simple and legible.
- Use professional business-letter format.
- Do not send your query letter bound in a folder, binder, or other fancy wrapper.
- Pitch only one project per letter.
- Use standard business envelopes or mailers. Keep it simple and professional.
- Send your query via first-class mail unless you would like to track delivery (using FedEx or UPS).

Let's take a look the elements that make up a successful query letter.

Provide an Overview of Your Book

1. Include a one-sentence hook.
2. Include a brief description of the book (one paragraph at most).
3. Be intriguing and persuasive, but avoid hyperbole and cliché.
4. Select a creative, catchy title for your book project.
5. Be sure to make a note of the manuscript's word count.
6. Identify who you think is the ideal audience for your book. The audience for the YA novel ranges from ages twelve to eighteen. Some manuscripts are ideal for the younger end of that range, and the edgier the novel, the older the audience.
7. Be cautious when comparing your project to well-known published works. Not only the topic, but the writing style should be similar when making a comparison. Never disparage another author's book.
8. Avoid using rhetorical questions as an introduction to your query letter.

9. Pique the agent's interest regarding your work immediately. You don't need to state the fact that you are seeking representation for your book.

The Bio: Describe Yourself as It Pertains to the Book Project

1. Briefly describe your education and writing experience.
2. If you have a well-read blog or have published articles, short stories, and other works, mention them.
3. Include work and personal experiences only if they are relevant to the topic of your book project. If you have credentials that qualify you for writing young adult books, be sure to list them. For example, you work with teens in a group home, or you are affiliated with a nonprofit organization that targets young people.
4. Do not explain the process by which you have written the book or your previous (and unsuccessful) attempts to find an agent or get your book published.

Contact Information

1. Always include a self-addressed stamped envelope.
2. Include your email address. This is usually the first way an editor or agent will respond to you.
3. In addition, include your physical address and phone number within your query letter.
4. As a courtesy, indicate whether you are submitting to multiple agents.

Other Materials (Depending on the Agent Guidelines)

1. Synopsis: Briefly describe the book's subject and provide a sense of its structure. Keep it brief—one page.
2. Sample pages or chapter: Unless this is specifically discouraged within the submission requirements, include a couple of pages or a whole chapter.

3. Avoid sending CD-ROMs or requesting that the agent download your project from a website. Agents typically do not want to download and print your materials. Also many editors are now using e-readers for their submissions and prefer to review materials as a Microsoft Word document.

FORMATTING A DOCUMENT FOR SUBMISSION IN MICROSOFT WORD

If you succeed in getting past the query stage, it's time to prepare your manuscript submission. Be sure to follow the guidelines provided by your agent or editor. If they do not provide guidelines, the following are acceptable specifications.

- **Header:** 0.5 inch with the title of the novel and your name on the left side and the number of pages on the right side.
- **Margins:** 1 inch all around
- **Line spacing:** Double or multiple for body text, single in long quotes
- **Lines per page:** 24 or 25
- **Font:** Times New Roman or Courier (do not mix)
- Use a different font only if it is essential to the story (rare).
- **Font size:** 12
- **Right margin:** Ragged
- **Left margin:** Justified
- Insert a page break instead of a series of returns at the end of a chapter or section.
- **Pagination:** Start chapter headings at the top of a new page.
- Don't start a new chapter partway down the page.
- **Paragraph indent:** 5 spaces, auto (don't type five blank spaces)
- **Exclamation points:** Use sparingly, if at all, and try not to use more than one at a time.
- Don't use em dashes, and use colons and semicolons only in rare cases.

- Space only once after a sentence.
- Don't write in ALL CAPS, not even to SHOUT.
- Rarely underline.
- Italic is used for internal dialogue or emphasis, but don't mix the uses.

"!!"

- ADVICE FROM PUBLISHERS ROW -

Kat Brzozowski, associate editor at Thomas Dunne Books/ St. Martin's Press:

"Publisher fatigue can be different from reader fatigue. You should never abandon your concept because people are telling there's no market for it. I'm sure there could be a great paranormal fantasy. Instead, polish your manuscript to ensure that it's phenomenally good when the market comes your way."

GETTING TO YES

While you're waiting for a response from an agent, start building your profile as an author. Resources for promotion and publicity in the publishing world are very limited, so an agent will want a sense of how you plan to sell your book. Create a social media presence and build an audience for yourself on blogs dedicated to YA. In fact, write your own YA blog. If you self-published your book, publishers will want to know how aggressively you sold it. If you don't have a publicity campaign ready, being creating one. The reality is that you are going to have to sell your book to the public. Being able to write is good, but being able to write and sell your book is better. The more you are able to demonstrate that you are willing to put in extra effort to attract sales, the more attractive your book will look to an agent.

CHAPTER 13

YA NONFICTION AND NEW ADULT

The publishing market is always changing, and new genres are constantly emerging. Suppose you'd like to write for the YA market, but the story you're compelled to tell really happened. Or, suppose you have a story that will appeal to youth, but feel your audience may be a little too old for the YA market. Fortunately, there are markets for those stories as well. This chapter will show you how to reach out to them through the genres of YA Nonfiction and New Adult.

YA NONFICTION: WHAT IS NONFICTION?

The standard definition for nonfiction is factual material that incorporates real people or actual events, or provides practical suggestions on a topic.

In general, publishers generally divide nonfiction into two categories. The first is narrative nonfiction, which tells a story based on factual events. Narrative nonfiction is designed to expand the reader's knowledge of a time period. Some recent YA examples are *The Nazi Hunters: How a Team of Spies and Survivors Captured the World's Most Notorious Nazi* by Neal Bascomb; *Imprisoned: The Betrayal of Japanese Americans During World War II* by Martin W. Sandler; and *The President Has Been Shot! The Assassination of John F. Kennedy* by James L. Swanson. Like fiction, these books have rising action and tension, build to a climax, and resolve to a conclusion. Think of narrative nonfiction as information interwoven with story. Readers should come away from narrative nonfiction having learned something about a significant topic, person, period, or event.

The other category is prescriptive nonfiction, where information is presented to the reader in a step-by-step approach designed to teach how to do something. It is practical advice about a skill or concept that can be applied to your life; think of it as a how-to guide that elucidates a topic. It may offer strategies, resources, or advice on a given subject. Recent examples include *The 6 Most Important Decisions You'll Ever Make* by Sean Covey; *The Teen's Guide to World Domination: Advice on Life, Liberty, and the Pursuit of Awesomeness* by Josh Shipp; and *How to Be Richer, Smarter, and Better-Looking Than Your Parents* by Zac Bissonnette. Prescriptive nonfiction may include occasional examples, but it centers on teaching the reader something different.

Publishers have taken a renewed interest in YA nonfiction, recognizing that there is a hungry audience for it. In addition, as schools are now adopting the Common Core standards—educational benchmarks designed to ensure all students in the nation have a comprehensive set of skills—great opportunities have opened up for editors to publish and sell books that incorporate core topics. The fact that, as of March 2014, forty-three of fifty states have implemented the Common Core means the school and library market has assumed greater importance in the publishing world. Editors are actively looking for YA nonfiction (as well as YA fiction that can be used in an educational setting). This explains the increase in the number of nonfiction titles being purchased.

"!!"

- ADVICE FROM PUBLISHERS ROW -

Daniel Ehrenhaft, editorial director at Soho Teen:

"We have educator's guides and a Common Core-aligned curriculum with material that teachers can use to teach the book. We're really excited about that, and develop our educator's guides internally with the author's help."

The existence of the Common Core points to an essential difference between adult nonfiction and YA nonfiction. While nonfiction can be—and ideally is—entertaining, there is an additional educational component to YA nonfiction. The ideal YA nonfiction is informational, practical, and has curricular connections. This means YA editors are more likely to look for writing that can also be used in the classroom. Since books tied to topics learned in school can be intimidating in subject and presentation, the challenge is to write fascinating, well-written books on educational topics. If your book can promote and stimulate conversation both in and out of the classroom environment, so much the better.

Since nonfiction with strong educational leanings is something editors are looking for, let me provide a few tips for writing YA nonfiction. Writing YA nonfiction books requires expertise in a given subject, the ability to do intense research, and the skill to practically and creatively shape a broad base of information into an entertaining and engaging narrative that teens can relate to.

NARRATIVE NONFICTION

With narrative nonfiction, you want a richly detailed account of a time in history; your work should transport the reader to another place. Novelist L. P. Hartley said, "The past is a foreign country: they do things differently there." Exceptional YA nonfiction should expose youth to that foreign country, forcing them to juxtapose historical ideas, cultural norms, and interactions with today's world. The lives of people can shed light on the unexplored. Writing narrative nonfiction in particular requires a disciplined presentation rooted with historical facts. Your book should inspire young people to learn more about the time period or other relevant tie-ins to the topic.

What kinds of topics make for superb YA narrative nonfiction, besides those that are designed for educational utility? Unsurprisingly, they're the same topics that make any book—YA or not, narrative nonfiction or not—worth reading: readable history wed to an entertaining story. It's always worthwhile to explore what no one else has, as agents and editors are always looking for solid treatments that will introduce young readers to a fascinating subject. Put a fresh spin on a well-known incident; there's usually a mesmerizing story behind the story somewhere. After all, people plucked from obscurity have shaped history and there are many unheard of, improbable yet true stories that merit attention. So let's look at some narrative nonfiction categories.

Our History, Ourselves

History is a difficult subject to interest teenagers in, as many feel that these subjects are too closely knit to things they have to learn in school. But with such a wide breadth of topics, there's always room for a book with a refreshing new spin on an aspect of history that can capture the imagination of youth. One recent successful YA history book is *The Port Chicago 50: Disaster, Mutiny, and the Fight for Civil Rights* by Steve Sheinkin. Appealing a little bit more to the younger end of the YA audience, this book depicts an incident where fifty black naval sailors went on strike over unsafe working conditions, were charged with mutiny, and faced possible execution.

Subjects ripe for exploration are events and topics that are close to a century old or more—subjects teenagers can hardly imagine in their world today. For example, *The Great American Dust Bowl* by Don Brown introduces teens to the crippling drought that wreaked havoc during the 1930s. Young people may be dimly aware that the Dust Bowl was the setting of *The Grapes of Wrath*. However, Brown's use of visual media brings to life this time in history and vividly portrays the harrowing stories of heartache and grief beyond the realm of Steinbeck's famous novel. Another instance is *Bomb: The Race to Build—and Steal—the World's Most Dangerous Weapon* by Steve Sheinkin. This book reveals the plotting, the risk, the deception, and the genius that created what is still the world's most formidable weapon.

In *An American Plague: The True and Terrifying Story of the Yellow Fever Epidemic of 1793* by Jim Murphy, an epidemic of yellow fever in Philadelphia is portrayed in a fascinating true story of a city under siege, spotlighting timely parallels to modern-day epidemics. Given that the worst of the AIDS pandemic is rapidly becoming a memory, this book illustrates how an outbreak of a disease can impact politics. In this case, a constitutional crisis arose when President Washington was forced to leave the Philadelphia due to the spread of yellow fever.

Historically marginalized populations are a terrific avenue for YA nonfiction, simply because they provide an avenue to introduce fresh stories to readers. One recent example is *Courage Has No Color: The True Story of the Triple Nickles, America's First Black Paratroopers* by Tanya Lee Stone. This book, which won multiple awards—including the NAACP Image Award—examines the history of the brave soldiers who fought in an obscure attack on the American West by the Japanese. Stories like these unearth the hidden histories that have molded America.

Like Sand Through the Hourglass, So Are the Days of Our Lives

Most biographies feature well-known people. YA nonfiction often features past presidents. Take, as a case in point, *Emancipation Proclamation: Lincoln and the Dawn of Liberty* by Tonya Bolden. Instead of concentrating on the whole of Lincoln's life, Bolden revives interest in Lincoln's legacy by focusing on his passage of the Emancipation Proclamation. If you are able to examine a unique element of a famous historical figure's life, there is a market out there for your book.

Of course, there is always room for an excellent biography on a well-known individual, as *Master of Deceit: J. Edgar Hoover and America in the Age of Lies* by Marc Aronson proves. Hoover's pursuit of "security at all costs," raises relevant points about the post-9/11 world. Good biographies are able to make the subject relevant, not just to their own time, but to ours as well.

I Am Woman, Hear Me Roar

As I mentioned, giving voice to and uncovering the stories of an underrepresented people is a superb way of finding a compelling story to tell. Biographies of groups—in this case, groups of women—can provide fertile ground for compelling, relevant narratives. *Pure Grit: How American World War II Nurses Survived Battle and Prison Camp in the Pacific* by Mary Cronk Farrell shines a light on how American nurses were treated up to and including on the Bataan Death March. By shining a spotlight on a previously unknown aspect of World War II, this book contains moving recollections of several of the nurses that bring the story to life.

Another technique for telling compelling stories is to put together a compendium of various historical figures, as in *Historical Heartthrobs: 50 Timeless Crushes—from Cleopatra to Camus* by Kelly Murphy and Hallie Fryd. Another is *Women in Space: 23 Stories of First Flights, Scientific Missions, and Gravity-Breaking Adventures* by Karen Bush Gibson. Be aware, however, that your concept isn't stretched too thin. The key to making these type of stories work is finding a common connection between the figures and tying them together with a great hook. The reader should be drawn to the topic with the promise delivered in the title. Who wouldn't be drawn to mad, bad, and dangerous to know types or drawn into love and romance throughout the ages? Or chilled to the bone by stories of deadly *femme fatales*?

Never feel that you have to limit yourself to the stories that weave in a collective. Recent YA nonfiction books have focused on an individual woman as well. *The Girl from the Tar Paper School: Barbara Rose Johns and the Advent of the Civil Rights Movement* by Teri Kanefield shares a critical though obscure story of how Barbara Johns, a high school junior, led a strike for equal facilities in her town's schools. *Claudette Colvin: Twice Toward Justice* by Phillip M. Hoose explores the story of Claudette Colvin, a key plaintiff in the court case that struck down segregation laws in Montgomery, Alabama. Mr. Hoose was particularly lucky, as he was able to interview Ms. Colvin herself. In fact, Ms. Colvin actively promoted the book and made media appearances with Mr. Hoose. If, like Mr. Hoose, you have access to your subject, use him or her! Ms. Colvin's unique cooperation in her own life story may have led to her biography winning the National Book Award Winner for Young People's Literature and being a 2010 Newbery Honor Book.

However, if you're writing about an individual's life, make sure to show how her life reflects her cultural milieu. For example, in Tonya Bolden's *Searching for Sarah Rector: The Richest Black Girl in America*, the story of the woman who discovered oil in Oklahoma is interwoven with multiple threads of U.S. history, among them slavery, Native American policy, and westward expansion. Paying homage to your subject is important, but remember that he or she didn't live in a vacuum. Biographies should capture a story, but don't forget to give historical context of your subject so people can better understand why his or her life mattered.

And the Rest Is History

Cultural history is a record and interpretation of past events involving human beings through the social, cultural, and political lenses of or relating to the arts and manners that a group favors. Most people may think of cultural history books as a recent development, but *The Story of Mankind* by Hendrik Willem van Loon won the Newbery Award, given to the most distinguished contribution to American literature for children, in 1922. This book has been updated many times, most recently in the winter of 2013, and still remains a phenomenon. One recent captivating example is *Expressing the Inner Wild: Tattoos, Piercings, Jewelry, and Other Body Art* by Stephen G. Gordon, an enthralling account of how humans have modified their bodies throughout history.

Since culture is nebulously defined, its topics are frequently diverse. One common element, though, is concentrating on an idea that's persisted throughout history and multiple cultures. *Buried Beneath Us: Discovering the Ancient Cities of the Americas* by Anthony Aveni is solid treatment of a fascinating subject, talking about ancient civilizations of the Americas and how they are relevant today. Its spotlight on early American civilizations pointedly addresses what can be learned from the rise and fall of civilizations.

You Animal, You

Humans aren't the only animal that YA nonfiction focuses on. After all, science is changing our world all the time. Science books like *The Dolphins of Shark Bay* by Pamela S. Turner help readers expand their erudition of the natural world by showing dolphins at play, hunting, herding, and fighting. Thought-provoking books like these open doors for youth, especially those who took an interest in animals growing up.

Science books can also help explain the behavior of animals as the world encroaches upon their natural habitats, as in *Wild Animal Neighbors: Sharing Our Urban World* by Ann Downer. Teens are often encouraged to think about volunteering opportunities and ways to help our world. Some books have even tied themselves to charities designed to save the planet or endangered species. Downer's book does a great job at offering suggestions for teens who are concerned about the environment.

Sometimes, science books can open up a new career to teenagers. *Navy SEAL Dogs: My Tale of Training Canines for Combat* by Michael Ritland portrays the world of dog training to teens. The author's work with the Warrior Dog Foundation reveals fascinating insights as to what dog signals mean. It also makes public how the failed search for weapons of mass destruction in Iraq led to the formation of an elite K-9 unit.

All three of these books tie into important topics in today's world—biology, environmentalism, and terrorism. Science books with a strong educational aspect are attractive properties in publishing today, so bear that in mind when selecting a subject.

Root, Root, Root for the Home Team

With sports, while there's always room for another book on traditional sports such as football, baseball, and basketball, there's something unique about the book *Ultimate Fighting: The Brains and Brawn of Mixed Martial Arts* by Patrick Jones. It gives a bird's-eye look at a sport that combines multiple fighting styles, including karate, boxing, kickboxing, wrestling, Vale Tudo, Muay Thai, and Brazilian Jiu-Jitsu. Young people involved in the X Games have even motivated the International Olympic Committee to think outside the box as it relates to sports. Most recently, the 2014 Winter Olympics introduced twelve new sports. Why not consider one of these recent additions?

As is true for history books, looking for unexplored stories can be fertile ground for a heart-wrenching narrative. In *In These Girls, Hope Is a Muscle*, Madeleine Blais recounts the story of the Amherst Lady Hurricanes, a scrappy, tough-playing high school girls' basketball team. Through detailing their 1992–1993 season, Blais also notes a sea change in high school policies, as the team's town supported its female athletes in a way previously reserved for male athletes. The best sports stories can be a window into the national consciousness.

A Pictures Says a Thousand Words

Graphic novels, where stories are rendered artistically, are extremely popular, but who says graphic storytelling should be limited to fiction? *Bad for You: Exposing the War on Fun!* by Kevin C. Pyle and Scott Cunningham is one of many books reinventing the graphic genre. Their book exposes a catalog of party poopers, from Anthony Comstock to the wet blankets who opposed *Harry Potter*.

Some subjects lend themselves to the graphic approach more than others. Take, for example, *Growing Up, Inside and Out* by Kira Vermond, illustrated by Carl Chin. It tackles the evergreen subject of puberty, both physically and mentally, with frank talk about crushes, gender identity, and sexual orientation. Its pictures emphasize its modern approach, showing a half-dressed couple looking at a condom wrapper at one point. If pictures will help illustrate your points, then consider using graphics with your material.

In other cases, the subject is impossible to divorce from a pictorial approach. In *Go: A Kidd's Guide to Graphic Design* by Chip Kidd, pictures are the whole point! The book introduces teens to the fundamentals of design in an engaging, colorful style. The book also allows teens to experiment with what they've learned, providing ten design projects at the end. In addition to allowing young people to develop their own visual distinctiveness, *Go* uses design elements to creatively emphasize key concepts. If your subject touches upon art or other visual elements, then a graphic scheme might be the best way to reach your audience.

When I Was Your Age

Memoir can open a teen's world to experiences they'll never have directly. For instance, not every teen is going to spend their life preparing for the Rapture, but that's exactly what Aaron Hartzler's *Rapture Practice* is about. On the other hand, teenagers will be able to connect to experiences his parents would never approve of, such as listening to popular music, planning debauched and drunken parties, and a burgeoning attraction to other boys. By wrapping a tale of adolescent upheaval inside an unfamiliar setting, teens will encounter something both ordinary and extraordinary.

Sometimes the unusual backdrop of a memoir is a historical event of major importance. In *March: Book One* by John Lewis, Lewis, one of the original Freedom Riders, recalls events ranging from meeting Martin Luther King Jr. and joining sit-ins in 1960 Nashville to Barack Obama's first inauguration. In this case, young people, who will probably be aware of racial injustice, will see that theme personally applied to the historical events that John Lewis lived through.

The strange social backdrop of a memoir, however, doesn't necessarily have to be something historical; it can be an issue that affects people today. In *Enrique's Journey: The True Story of a Boy Determined to Reunite with His Mother* by Sonia Nazario, the harrowing journey of one illegal alien's trek to America gives the reader palpable chills. By forthrightly addressing the hazards Enrique faced—beatings, rape, maiming, and murder—readers gain a new perspective on the subject of illegal immigration.

Another example is *Hidden Girl: The True Story of a Modern-Day Child Slave* by Shyima Hall and Lisa Wysocky. Sold by her parents at age eight and then illegally trafficked into the United States, Shyima Hall tells her story to draw attention to a growing global crisis. This memoir puts a human face on the issue of trafficking, candidly addressing issues that no teenager should ever face.

Sometimes, mixing genres can lead to a truly creative approach for a difficult subject. David Small used graphic nonfiction to write *Stitches*, his memoir of being transformed into a mute. This National Book Award finalist pictorially represents a fantastic descent into adolescent hell and the authors' hard emotional and artistic road to recovery.

FYI

Information books can take a difficult topic and make it palatable for teens to learn about it. Take, for instance, *Beyond Magenta: Transgender Teens Speak Out* by Susan Kuklin. In this book, verbal and visual profiles elucidate what it's like to identify fully as female or male, to identify as neither male nor female, or to be intersex. By focusing on the process of transitioning and not on genitalia, this book sensitively addresses subject matter that is too often sensationalized.

In other cases, informational books can present information readers need to know in a creative way. In *Everybody Paints! The Lives and Art of the Wyeth Family* by Susan Goldman Rubin, design elements such as changing fonts and background color draw attention to the oeuvre of this creative clan. In doing so, teens who aren't familiar with the artwork of the Wyeth kin will come away with a sense of their importance in the American art scene.

And the Beat Goes On

Given the wide range of music itself, it shouldn't surprise you of the wide range of possible music topics. "Gangnam Style" swept the nation in 2012, providing the backdrop for *K-Pop: Korea's Musical Explosion* by Stuart A. Kallen. By focusing on the last twenty years, the book profiles the most influential artists while describing the antiquated Korean studio system. A revealing look at the Korean music scene for newbies, this book gives readers a rudimentary knowledge of Korean culture and its pop music scene.

The American music scene also provides fertile ground to cover. *Legends, Icons & Rebels: Music That Changed the World* by Robbie Robertson,

Jim Guerinot, Sebastian Robertson, and Jared Levine covers twenty-seven thoughtfully selected musicians known for their radical experimentation with music. In choosing such a small sample, books of this type spark debate as to who has been included or excluded and why. A CD of music samples helps pique the curiosity of readers to whom these musicians are unknown.

Of course, the most well-known musical story of all time is still yielding new stories. In *How the Beatles Changed the World* by Martin W. Sandler, the progress of Beatlemania is tracked and the band's influence on record singles, record albums, album covers, and cultural zeitgeist is noted. With chapters on the Beatles' fashion, hairstyles, and movies, this book makes the case that the Beatles did, in fact, change the world.

PRESCRIPTIVE NONFICTION: HOW DO I...

Until now, we've been talking about narrative nonfiction, which blends story with factual information. Let's switch gears and talk about prescriptive nonfiction, which teaches the reader how to do something. Genres of prescriptive nonfiction vary widely. Cooking and food-related books are fairly common, such as *The Smart Girl's Guide to Going Vegetarian: How to Look Great, Feel Fabulous, and Be a Better You* by Rachel Meltzer Warren. By helping teens identify their own personal values, Warren's book guides potential vegetarians toward the lifestyle best suited for them.

Some topics may be timelier than others. In school students are taught how to write, but some teens may, like you, be interested in honing their craft so they can write for a wider audience. *Thrice Told Tales: Three Mice Full of Writing Advice* by Catherine Lewis acquaints readers with various literary styles by rewriting one nursery rhyme repeatedly. By tackling everything from style to swearing, this book is short, clever, witty, and—most of all—fun to read.

Another relevant subject to teens is answering the question,

"What do I want to be when I grow up?" Books that help young people explore various options can prove useful. *So, You Want to Be a Chef? How to Get Started in the World of Culinary Arts* by J. M. Bedell offers profiles of food industry careers and provides a comprehensive introduction to the food business. Food service professionals share their insights and offer advice about choosing a culinary arts career.

Teenagers are also full of insecurities and want help dealing with them. Enter books like *Scared Stiff: Everything You Need to Know About 50 Famous Phobias* by Sara Latta. Part entertainment, part therapy, this book helps teens know they're not alone by including celebrity co-sufferers and offering a warm, optimistic tone.

A NOTE TO THE WISE

So now that we've covered possible avenues for your YA nonfiction book, what advice can I give you? I want to stress the importance of an Author's Note—teens are going to want to know how you came up with the idea. So tell them! Don't skimp; let them know how your concept began, what your research was like, and why you felt your subject was important. If your focus is truly fascinating, then teens are going to want to know everything they can about it. In addition, be sure to include what you hope they'll learn from it; this can also be a yardstick by which you measure the success of your book.

Another important thing to remember is that we've moved into a transmedia culture, so be sure to include any maps, photos, technological references, or diagrams that are important to your research. And don't forget to post your bibliography on your website; some readers may want to follow in your footsteps and research the topic on their own. It doesn't hurt to include bibliographical information at the end of your book, but it's often best to place it on your website—this way, you can stay tied to your readership.

But the most important advice I can offer about writing nonfiction is to *pick a topic that interests you*. If you're passionate about your topic, then that excitement will transfer to the book and, eventually, your readers. Don't select a topic that doesn't interest you based on how well you think it will sell; that's a recipe for a dull, pedantic book no one will want to read.

If you are writing a nonfiction book, then you need to know what agents will expect when you approach them. Typically, agents and editors who acquire nonfiction look for a proposal instead of a complete manuscript up front. A proposal introduces the topic to the agent or editor, details the author's expertise in the subject, and presents plans on how the book will reach its target audience. It's a business plan that attempts to sell a well-developed concept.

THE BOOK PROPOSAL

So you've decided you want to write a nonfiction book for the YA market. Great! You're going to need a query letter and a book proposal. (Please refer to Chapter 12 for how to format a query letter.) Now, let me walk you through the elements of a nonfiction book proposal.

- **Marketing and publishing rationale:** Why do you think this book is needed in the marketplace? Who will benefit and why? Why have you chosen to write it?

  The marketing and publishing rationale needs to make the case that there is a strong commercial need for this book. It should show that this book fills a gap in the market somehow—maybe one that the public isn't even aware of yet.

- **Audience:** Who are you publishing to? Why would they be interested in purchasing your book?

  You may feel that everybody needs your book, but I can assure you, not everybody is going to buy it. Have a strong sense of who will be interested in your book and why. Be specific. If you're writing for YA, think about who might be interested in the topic—athletes, Latinos, kids in rural areas? Be able to justify why your book will interest your chosen audience.

- **Brief description:** A one- to three-sentence summary of the book. Think of this as potential back cover copy.

Imagine that your book is about to be published; if you were going to pick it up off the shelf of your local bookstore, what would it say on the back? Remember, your space is limited, so you've really got to grab a reader's attention. Your brief description should clearly communicate the book's concept and draw in a potential reader.

- **Book description/chapter outline:** A clear description of what the book is and what it's trying to achieve. This will include a table of contents, chapter heads, and a brief description of each chapter.

This is the meat of your proposal. Think of it as the blueprint of how your book will develop. Each chapter should have a brief summary, showing how it relates to the book's overall concept.

- **Key features and selling points:** A concise, bulleted list of key reasons why readers will want to pick up the book.

If you only had thirty seconds to tell someone what they would learn from reading your book, what would you say? What points would you want them to know? Does your book capitalize on any current trends? Consider that when writing your key features and selling points. It can help you effectively communicate exactly what you hope to teach.

- **Author platform and bio:** A profile that includes information that will help the publisher understand why you are the ideal person to write this book.

As fascinating as your childhood hobbies may be to you, that's not what agents or editors are looking for when they read your bio. They want to know that an audience is clamoring to hear what you have to say. So think strategically when preparing your bio—what does your online presence look like? How many Twitter followers do you have? Have you been published previously? Do you have any media connections? Are you comfortable on camera? What plans do you have to get your book discovered by your audience? Hopefully, your platform and bio will answer these questions.

- **Marketing/publicity plan:** Do you have any special relationship to the market? Are there any special conferences, trade shows, or magazines that your book would be an ideal candidate for?

Now that the agent or editor knows you're an expert in the field, you have to prove that you have the ability to sell this book to its audience. Think of this section of the proposal as a way to demonstrate that you have the requisite ability and media connections to get people talking about your book, and that realistic opportunities exist to promote it.

- **Competition or related titles:** What are some other published titles that resemble your concept or discuss the same topic? How do those books fall short in comparison? How does your title offer a different approach?

No matter how unique and different your book is, there will always be titles it competes against. The comparative works should show that there is a market for your book, but you also need to explain how your book will distinguish itself from the crowd. You'll probably come across some competitive titles in your research, but you can also search for competitive titles on Amazon or Goodreads and at your local library. Once you have found one title, Amazon has a feature that identifies other books similar in topic. This is a great starting point for finding other comparative titles. Be sure to include enough information to identify your competition—author, title, publisher, page count and publication date.

This may be the most important section of the proposal because it's how an editor or agent will determine how much your book is worth. Typically, agents or editors will look up the books you've listed in Bookscan—a program through the Nielsen company—to see how many units these works have sold. After getting a sense of how well books like yours sell, they will use these figures to help determine how much money they will offer you for your book.

- **Book specifications:** How long do you expect your book to be? Do you anticipate any unusual features, like charts, maps, or graphs? How long do you think it will take you to deliver a complete manuscript?

  If your book will feature color photography or a nonstandard printing format, now is the time to let the agent or editor know. When specifying length, don't get caught up trying to figure out the page count—the approximate word count will suffice.

The elements above are staples of most proposals, but bear in mind that your proposal must be uniquely customized. Some agents may have their own proposal guidelines, so make sure that you proposal meets their requirements. Remember, your proposal needs to be a window into the personality of your work. Make it engaging, informative, and representative of the voice and tone of your book as a whole.

NEW ADULT: AN EXCITING NEW MARKET

For years, when authors would call my office, I'd tell them that the age range for the YA market was fourteen to twenty-four. This isn't necessarily true anymore. Readers who grew up on YA are now looking for books that have the same dynamic intensity of YA but deal with the realities of making one's way in the world. To accommodate this new audience, a genre called New Adult is catering to the needs of this market.

So what exactly is New Adult, and how does it differ from YA? The term was first coined in 2009 by St. Martin's Press when it held a special call for "fiction similar to YA that can be published and marketed as adult—a sort of an 'older YA' or 'new adult.'" As YA readers aged out of the genre, publishers needed a way to maintain a connection to those readers. So New Adult was created to generate both books for those readers and a space on the bookshelf for those stories.

Of course, that sounds altruistic, but New Adult is also a marketing tool. It's a means to market to and retain the reading loyalty of adults of all ages who enjoy the expressive fervor of YA books.

So, let's imagine that you've got a story to tell, but you aren't sure whether your audience falls under Young Adult or New Adult. How do you determine your story's market? According to Jessica Sinsheimer, associate agent at Sarah Jane Freymann Literary Agency, if your characters are in high school and dealing with high school problems, then your manuscript is YA. If your protagonist is slightly older and trying to transition into adulthood, then you're writing for the New Adult market. Covers for New Adult books tend to be more sexualized as well—a little less brooding and more explicit than YA covers.

Genres are always rather elastic, and New Adult needs time to evolve. But what can we say about it in its infancy? Let's look at some common elements in today's New Adult market.

- Remember all the experiences of life after high school? Moving away to college, buying your first car, working your way through school, getting your first job, moving out, office romances, internships, travel abroad, military deployment, and first apartments, among other things? A lot of monumental firsts happen between eighteen and twenty-five—the age of the New Adult reader.

  New Adult books focus on the heady post–high school,

pre–late twenties years when young people are establishing their independence and becoming more settled adults. They reflect the challenges of moving out, forging careers, and negotiating education and career choices.

- Since a lot of the characters in New Adult novels are college age, a lot of New Adult novels involve a college setting. For example, there's *Fangirl* by Rainbow Rowell, a novel about a woman whose twin sister does not want to share a room at college; *Beautiful Disaster* by Jamie McGuire, about a woman's bet with the campus lothario; and *Losing It* by Cora Carmack, about a college senior who's determined to lose her virginity before she graduates. If high school is a common element in YA books, college is the corresponding element in New Adult books.

- There is no doubt that YA has become increasingly edgy, especially regarding sexuality. Like it or not, we live in a hypersexualized world. But as the age for New Adult is older than YA, any residual modesty that existed in a YA manuscript is gone in the New Adult marketplace.

  This doesn't mean you must fill your manuscript with orgies aplenty! After all, New Adult isn't simply sexed-up YA. However, an increase in reader maturity necessitates an increase in material maturity. You're going to have to ramp up the raciness. In fact, your readers will expect it—Ericka Clay at tipsylit.com complained that New Adult books didn't have enough erotic content in them. So be advised—keep it steamy!

- Since New Adult is a recent publishing development, it's still grappling with its identity. Instead of being relegated to children's imprints, adult fiction editors have been publishing New Adult, usually under a romance imprint. Therefore, there's been a strong bias toward New Adult fiction with a romantic element. One example is *Rush Me* by Allison Parr, about a young woman's romance with a professional football player. Another example is *Headfirst Falling* by Melissa Guinn, about a woman who struggles with her feelings for her brother's fellow soldier.

While there's certainly a lot of overlap between contemporary romance and New Adult, there are important differences between the two genres. Contemporary romance tends to use third-person point of view, while New Adult generally has a first-person narrator, in order to keep the voice and style that it shares with YA. Contemporary romance also tends to deal with major life events, such as marriage and pregnancy. New Adult relationships tend not to have the same sense of gravity. That's not to say New Adult books that deal with marriage and pregnancy can't be done, but if you do pursue that path, keep your tone consistent with the New Adult market.

- New Adult may have originally been published under romance imprints, but it is rapidly coming into its own. Random House has already created its first exclusive New Adult imprint, Flirt, and other imprints are sure to follow. But New Adult books are branching out beyond the romance genre. Romantic suspense titles like *Beautiful Player* by Christina Lauren and *Rebel* by Elle Casey are stretching New Adult's boundaries and giving authors more leeway to experiment. Jamie Maguire's next book, *Red Hill*, is a New Adult novel set against a zombie apocalypse. While we haven't seen New Adult science fiction pop up yet, I'm sure it's on the horizon.

So don't restrict yourself to romantic stories or feel that no editors will want to read a New Adult steampunk novel revolving around a series of gruesome murders. They might! The New Adult market needs pioneers and originality. It's up to you to start trends and open doors.

- I don't know if you've been paying attention, but so far, all of the books I've mentioned have female protagonists. That has not been a conscious choice on my part. Most of the literature around New Adult mentions novels with female protagonists. I suppose that's why New Adult is often misperceived as sexed-up chick lit.

Making Faces, by Amy Harmon, features both male and female protagonists. But the fact that I could only find one New Adult novel with a male lead character mentioned in all the reading I did points to a serious gender imbalance. It also indicates a critically untapped market. Feel free to push the boundaries of New Adult with daring, challenging male protagonists. You could be the one who opens up a bold new frontier in the New Adult market.

So should you write for the New Adult market? Absolutely! If you have a story that will appeal to a slightly older market, I encourage you to write it. Don't let the fact that the genre is new or that your book doesn't seem to fit exact categories stop you. As I said earlier, the market is expanding and genre is always shifting. Just bear in mind that many of the same rules apply in New Adult books— whatever your market, you need realistic characters, a compelling plot, and vividly drawn settings to successfully find an audience.

ENVOI

Medieval poets used to end many of their poems with an envoi, a short stanza at the end of a poem addressed to an imagined or actual person that commented on the preceding poem.

Consider this my envoi to you, wrapped in good wishes for your writing future. I wish you believable, realistic, energetic characters who take you and your readers to places you never dreamed of going. I hope you craft stories that linger in your readers' minds long after they've finished your book and tightly woven plots that keep them turning the pages. May your settings be places your readers dream about visiting at night, and may your point of view challenge, inspire, and lead them deeper into your novel. I wish you the courage to be a ruthless and unflinching editor of your own work, to work with an agent who is enthusiastic about your manuscript, and to find a publisher who will bring it to as wide an audience as possible.

And lastly, may you have the joy of seeing your book on the bookshelves—and may I have the pleasure of reading it.

APPENDIX A

Feedback Resources

YA WRITING PROGRAMS

Hamline University: This is a low-residency program that offers an MFA in writing for children and young adults. It has one-to-one mentoring with the faculty. The program provides semiannual residencies each January and July where faculty and students gather for eleven days of intensive lectures, workshops, seminars, and readings devoted exclusively to writing for children and young adults. More information about the program can be found at www .hamline.edu/mfac/.

Spalding University: It provides a low-residency program that focuses on writing for children and young adults. Students may customize the location, season, and pace of their studies. You can find more information at spalding.edu/academics /mfa-in-writing/.

Hollins University: "Hollins offers summer MA and MFA programs exclusively in the study and writing of children's literature." See www.hollins.edu/grad/eng_writing/index.shtml.

Lesley University: It offers a low-residency MFA program in writing for young people. The ten-day residency begins each semester with seminars, workshops, readings, and the chance to design the semester's program of study. Students work independently during the semester under the guidance of their faculty mentor. The program also offers scholarships. Its web address is www.lesley.edu/gsass/creative_writing.

Simmons College: This is a full-time MFA program designed for students pursuing the MFA in writing for children. "MFA students take writing courses and work closely with a mentor to produce a manuscript from conception to submission." See more at www.simmons.edu/gradstudies/liberal-arts/academics/childrens-literature/writing.shtml.

Vermont College of Fine Arts: It offers a two-year low-residency MFA program in writing for children and young adults. "The program offers individualized education with faculty-guided independent-study projects." See www.vcfa.edu/wcya.

Writers Workshop at Chautauqua: This is a conference sponsored by the Highlights Foundation dedicated to children's and YA books. "It includes seminars, small-group workshops, and one-on-one sessions with prominent authors, illustrators, editors, critics, and publishers in the world of children's literature." See www.highlightsfoundation.org/upcoming-workshops/.

Antioch University: It offers a ten-day residency program with a concentration in writing for young people, featuring collaboration with illustrators, editors, and agents on the faculty. See www.antiochla.edu/academics/mfa-creative-writing/program-features/genres/.

Seton Hall University: It offers a low-residency program with modules focusing on YA and children's literature. Emphasis is on writing for the popular market. See www-2011.setonhill.edu/catalog/shucat/displaySection.cfm?&VID=39&SID=293&CID=2.

University of Nebraska, Omaha: This two-and-a-half-year low-residency program welcomes authors who are interested in YA. Residency is not in Omaha itself, but in nearby Nebraska City. See www.unomaha.edu/unmfaw/.

Columbia College: It offers a full-time program with a

concentration in writing for young people. Columbia College also offers two campus journals, *Hair Trigger* and *F Magazine*, for students to showcase their work. See www.colum.edu/Admissions/Graduate /programs/mfa-creative-writing-fiction-program/index.php.

Fairfield University: While this two-year low-residency program does not offer a concentration in YA, students are encouraged to write in this genre. See www.fairfield.edu/academics /schoolscollegescenters/collegeofartssciences/graduateprograms /mfaincreativewriting/.

Pine Manor College: Like Fairfield University, while this low-residency MFA program does not offer a concentration in writing for the YA market, students are encouraged to write in this genre. See www.pmc.edu/mfa.

Southern New Hampshire University: This university offers a low-residency MFA program with a concentration in writing YA literature and connections with editors, agents, and other publishing insiders. See www.snhu.edu/mfa-creative-writing.asp.

Whidbey Writers Workshop: This program offers both an MFA low-residency program with a concentration in writing children's and YA literature and residencies for writers who are not seeking an MFA. See www.nila.edu/mfa/.

YA BOOK REVIEWS

School Library Journal is a reviewer of books, multimedia, and technology for children. You can visit it online at www .schoollibraryjournal.com.

Kirkus Reviews publishes reviews of children's and young adult books two to three months before the publication date. The reviews are written by specialists selected for their knowledge and expertise in a particular field. Read the reviews at www.kirkusreviews.com.

Publishers Weekly is an international news website and magazine for book publishing and book selling that includes reviews, bestseller lists, commentary, and information for authors. Find it online at www.publishersweekly.com.

VOYA Magazine is a bimonthly magazine devoted to those who serve young adults. It includes articles about the informational needs of teenagers that may be helpful in writing and selling your manuscript. The website is www.voyamagazine.com/.

WEBSITES, BLOGS, AND OTHER ONLINE COMMUNITIES

Teenreads.com provides teens with information about authors, books, series, and characters. The site shares book reviews, author profiles and interviews, excerpts of new releases, and literary games and contests.

The Young Adult Library Services Association, found at www.ala.org/yalsa, is a division of the American Library Association dedicated to books for the young adult reader.

Jacketflap.com is a comprehensive resource for information on the children's book industry. It has a searchable database of information on children's and YA book publishers, agents, and editors.

YA Book Blog Directory is a list of YA book blogs. A comprehensive site of blogs dedicated to the YA market, it's an excellent reference for authors looking to publicize their books, publishers looking for reviewers, book bloggers looking to network, and teenage readers.

Many authors use blogs to promote their books; it's an excellent way to reach your audience and build excitement about your writing. Some authors even go on blog tours, where they visit a number of blogs, do interviews, and promote their book. So it's in your best interest to be familiar on as many online communities as possible.

AWARDS FOR THE YOUNG ADULT MARKET

The Michael L. Printz Award is an award for a book that exemplifies literary excellence in young adult literature. It is named for a Topeka, Kansas, school librarian who was a longtime active member of the Young Adult Library Services Association.

The William C. Morris Debut YA Award, first awarded in 2009, honors a debut book published by an author writing for teens and celebrates impressive new voices in young adult literature.

The National Book Award for Young People's Literature is administered by the National Book Foundation and recognizes the best in young people's literature annually.

The *Los Angeles Times* Book Prize for Young Adult Fiction was established in 1998 to recognize the best in young adult literature and is administered by the *Los Angeles Times*.

The Edgar Allan Poe Award for Best Young Adult Novel has become widely acknowledged to be one of the most prestigious awards in the genre of mystery. This award is sponsored by the Mystery Writers of America.

The Margaret A. Edwards Award was established in 1988 and honors an author, as well as a specific body of his or her work, for significant and lasting contribution to young adult literature. It recognizes an author's work in helping young people become aware of themselves and in addressing questions about their role and importance in relationships, society, and the world.

The YALSA (Young Adult Library Services Association) Award for Excellence in Nonfiction honors the best nonfiction book published for young adults (ages twelve through eighteen). The award winner is announced annually at the ALA Midwinter Meeting Youth Media.

YALSA also sponsors the **Alex Awards**, given to ten books written for adults that also appeal to young adults, ages twelve through eighteen. Margaret A. Edwards pioneered young adult library; her work is described in her book *Fair Garden and the Swarm of Beasts*. The Alex Awards are named after Edwards, who was called "Alex" by her friends.

The IRA (International Reading Association) Children's and Young Adults Book Award is intended for newly published authors who show unusual promise in the young adults book field. Awards are given for fiction and nonfiction, and books from all countries are considered, so long as they are published in English.

The Américas Award, sponsored by the national Consortium of Latin American Studies Programs, is given in recognition of U.S. works of fiction, poetry, folklore, or selected nonfiction published in English ,or Spanish that authentically and engagingly portray Latin America, the Caribbean, or Latinos in the United States.

The Mike Morgan and Larry Romans Young Adult Literature Award, sponsored by the Stonewall Book Awards, is awarded to exceptional young adult literature that portrays the gay, lesbian, bisexual, and transgender (GLBT) experience.

The Cybil Awards are given each year by bloggers for the year's best YA titles. Categories include YA speculative fiction, YA nonfiction, and YA fiction.

***

There are additional national and state awards. They can be found at www.cynthialeitichsmith.com/lit_resources/awards/nat_awards .html.

APPENDIX B

Publishing Process at a Glance

1. Author writes the manuscript.
2. Author revises the manuscript.
3. Author gets critiques and implements necessary changes.
4. Author submits queries to agents.
5. Author secures agent.
6. Author makes any changes per the agent's feedback.
7. Agent submits work to publishers.
8. Editor reads the manuscript and tells agent she is enamored and plans to share with the editorial board.
9. Editor shares the manuscript with the editorial board.
10. Editor prepares profit-and-loss statement for the book.
11. Editor contacts agent and makes an offer.
12. Agent shares offer with author.
13. Agent negotiates the terms of the offer with editor.
14. Agent reviews actual contract, makes additions and deletions to the clauses in agreement in the best interest of the author—for example, redlines—and sends it back to the publisher's legal counsel.
15. Editor sends final contract to agent.
16. Agent sends contract to author for signature.
17. Editor prepares editorial notes for author, and the author revises again.

18. Author submits final manuscript.

19. Editor reviews the manuscript and then prepares it for production.

20. Editors in production department copyedit and proofread the manuscript.

21. Editor sends copyedits to the author for review.

22. Author reviews last pass of manuscript after proof.

23. Editor prepares back cover copy, catalog copy, and other tools to sell the book.

24. Publicity department sends out galley copies to media for review.

25. Book is published and selling begins.

APPENDIX C

Glossary of YA Genres and Terms

ADVENTURE FICTION: fiction where an adventure, an exciting undertaking involving risk and physical danger, forms the main story line.

BIOGRAPHICAL FICTION: fiction where an author gives a fictional account of the life of a real person.

BIOGRAPHY: an account of someone's life written by someone else.

DYSTOPIAN FICTION: fiction set in a society characterized by mass poverty, squalor, suffering, or oppression that society has most often brought upon itself.

FAIRY TALES: a children's story about magical and imaginary beings and lands.

FANTASY FICTION: fiction characterized by highly fanciful or supernatural elements.

FRACTURED FAIRY TALES: traditional fairy tales, rearranged to create new plots with fundamentally different meanings or messages.

HISTORICAL FICTION: fiction characterized chiefly by an imaginative reconstruction of historical events and personages.

HISTORICAL MYSTERY FICTION: fiction set in a historical time period whose central plot involves the solving of a mystery or crime (usually murder).

HISTORICAL ROMANCE FICTION: fiction set in a historical time period whose central plot is a romance between one or more characters.

HORROR FICTION: fiction intended to frighten, scare, or startle its readers by inducing feelings of horror and terror.

HUMOROUS FICTION: fiction employing or showing humor to entertain its readers.

ILLUSTRATED FICTION: a hybrid narrative medium in which images and text work together to tell a story.

MAGIC REALISM FICTION: fiction where magic elements are a natural part in an otherwise mundane, realistic environment.

MYSTERY FICTION: fiction where a detective investigates and solves a crime mystery.

PARANORMAL FICTION: fiction set in a world/universe very much like ours, with some kind of supernatural or paranormal creatures (werewolves, vampires, ghosts, etc.).

PARANORMAL ROMANCE FICTION: fiction set in this world, but involving a romance between two people at least one of whom is some sort of paranormal creature or has paranormal abilities.

POETRY: creative work in which special intensity is given to the expression of feelings and ideas by the use of distinctive style and rhythm. Fiction that includes a series of poems that tell a story and have a narrative arc are called novels in verse.

POST-APOCALYPTIC FICTION: fiction that is concerned with the end of human civilization.

REALISTIC FICTION: fiction that deals with events that, while untrue, are not outside the realm of possibility.

ROMANCE FICTION: fiction whose primary focus is romantic love between two people and that has an emotionally satisfying and optimistic ending.

SCIENCE FICTION: fiction based on imagined future scientific or technological advances and frequently portraying space or time travel and life on other planets.

SEA ADVENTURE FICTION: fiction where an adventure, an exciting undertaking involving risk and physical danger, takes place at sea.

SPY FICTION: fiction involving espionage as an important context or plot device.

STEAMPUNK FICTION: fiction set in an alternative history of the nineteenth-century British Victorian era or American Wild West or in a fantasy world that similarly employs steam power.

URBAN FANTASY FICTION: fiction where fantastical elements—magic and/or strange creatures—are set in an urban environment where the city itself is a character.

VAMPIRE FICTION: fiction concerned primarily with the subject of vampires.

WAR FICTION: fiction where the primary action takes place in a field of armed combat or where the characters are preoccupied with preparations for, or recovery from, war.

APPENDIX D

YA Books-to-Film Chart

BOOK (SERIES) TITLE	AUTHOR	YEAR OF PUBLICATION	FILM TITLE	YEAR OF RELEASE	MOVIE STUDIO	SUBGENRE
The Wonderful Wizard of Oz	L. Frank Baum	1900	The Wizard of Oz	1939	MGM Studios	Fantasy
A Little Princess	Frances Hodgson Burnett	1905	The Little Princess	1939	20th Century Fox	Mystery
National Velvet	Enid Bagnold	1935		1945	MGM Studios	Drama
The Yearling	Marjorie Kinnan Rawlings	1938		1946	MGM	Historical
Treasure Island	Robert Louis Stevenson	1883		1950	Walt Disney Productions	Adventure
20,000 Leagues Under the Sea	Jules Verne	1870		1954	Walt Disney Productions	Science fiction, adventure
Old Yeller	Fred Gipson	1956		1957	Walt Disney Productions	Historical
Lottie and Lisa	Erich Kastner	1949	The Parent Trap	1961	Walt Disney Productions	Drama, humor
To Kill a Mockingbird	Harper Lee	1960		1962	Universal Pictures	Historical, drama
Go Ask Alice	Beatrice Sparks	1971		1973	Metromedia Producers Corporation (MPC)	Drama
The Apple Dumpling Gang	Jack Bickham	1971		1975	Walt Disney Productions	Historical

BOOK (SERIES) TITLE	AUTHOR	YEAR OF PUBLICATION	FILM TITLE	YEAR OF RELEASE	MOVIE STUDIO	SUBGENRE
Escape to Witch Mountain	Alexander H. Key	1968		1975	Walt Disney Productions	Science fiction
Forever	Judy Blume	1975		1978	EMI Television; Roger Gimbel Productions	Romance
The Black Stallion	Walter Farley	1941		1979	American Zoetrope	Adventure
Tex	S. E. Hinton	1979		1982	Walt Disney Productions	Drama
Rumble Fish	S. E. Hinton	1975		1983	American Zoetrope	Drama
Something Wicked This Way Comes	Ray Bradbury	1962		1983	Walt Disney Productions; Bryna Productions	Fantasy/horror
The Outsiders	S. E. Hinton	1967		1983	Zoetrope Studios	Drama
I Am the Cheese	Robert Cormier	1997		1983	Almi Pictures	Crime, mystery
The Neverending Story	Michael Ende	1979		1984	Warner Bros.	Fantasy
That Was Then, This Is Now	S. E. Hinton	1971		1985	Paramount Pictures	Drama
The Princess Bride	William Goldman	1973		1987	ACT III Communications	Fantasy/comedy
The Chocolate War	Robert Cormier	1974		1988	MCEG Sterling	Drama
White Fang	Jack London	1906		1991	Walt Disney Pictures	Adventure
Madame Doubtfire	Anne Fine	1987	Mrs. Doubrfire	1993	Blue Wolf Productions	Humor
Little Women	Louisa May Alcott	1868		1994	Columbia Pictures	Drama
Jumanji	Chris Van Allsburg	1981		1995	Interscope Communications; Teitler Film	Fantasy
I Know What You Did Last Summer	Lois Duncan	1973		1997	Mandalay Entertainment	Suspense, thriller
The Borrowers	Mary Nolton	1952		1997	Working Title Films	Fantasy

BOOK (SERIES) TITLE	AUTHOR	YEAR OF PUBLICATION	FILM TITLE	YEAR OF RELEASE	MOVIE STUDIO	SUBGENRE
Practical Magic	Alice Hoffman	1995		1998	Village Roadshow Pictures; Di Novi Pictures	Fantasy
Where the Heart Is	Billie Letts	1995		2000	Wind Dancer Films	Romance
The Princess Diaries	Meg Cabot	2000–2009		2001	Walt Disney Pictures; BrownHouse Productions	Humor, drama
Harry Potter series	J. K. Rowling	1997		2001–2011	Warner Bros.	Fantasy
Tuck Everlasting	Natalie Babbitt	1975		2002	Walt Disney Pictures; Scholastic Entertainment	Fantasy
About a Boy	Nick Hornby	1998		2002	StudioCanal; TriBeCa Productions; Working Title Films	Humor, drama
Holes	Louis Sachar	1998		2003	Walt Disney Pictures and Walden Media	Historical, fantasy
Big Fish: A Novel of Mythic Proportions	Christopher Paolini	1997	*Big Fish*	2003	Jinks/Cohen Company; The Zanuck Company; Tim Burton Productions	Fantasy
Freaky Friday	Mary Rodgers	1972		2003	Walt Disney Pictures	Drama, fantasy
That Summer; Someone Like You	Sarah Dessen	1996; 1998	*How to Deal*	2003	New Line Cinema (USA); Focus Features	Romance
The Cheetah Girls	Deborah Gregory	1999		2003–2008	Disney	commercial, humor
The Bad Beginning; The Reptile Room; The Wide Window	Lemony Snicket	1999–2000	*Lemony Snicket's A Series of Unfortunate Events*	2004	Nickelodeon Movies; Scott Rudin Productions	Mystery/ gothic fiction
Around the World in Eighty Days	Jules Verne	1873		2004	Walt Disney Pictures/ Walden Media	Adventure

BOOK (SERIES) TITLE	AUTHOR	YEAR OF PUBLICATION	FILM TITLE	YEAR OF RELEASE	MOVIE STUDIO	SUBGENRE
Ella Enchanted	Gail Carson Levine	1997		2004	Jane Startz Productions; Blessington Film Productions	Fantasy, romance
Speak	Laurie Halse Anderson	1999		2004	Showtime Networks Inc.	Drama
Confessions of a Teenage Drama Queen	Dyan Sheldon	1999		2004	Walt Disney Pictures	Chick lit
Queen Bees and Wannabees	Rosalind Wiseman	2002	Mean Girls	2004	SNL Studios	Self-help
The Earthsea series	Ursula K. Le Guin	1968-2001	(TV miniseries)	2004	The Sci-Fi Channel	High fantasy, adventure
Howl's Moving Castle	Diana Wynne Jones	1986		2005	Studio Ghibli	Fantasy
The Sisterhood of the Traveling Pants	Ann Brashares	2001		2005	Alcon Entertainment; 12th Street Productions; Di Novi Pictures	Drama
T*Witches	H. B. Gilmour and Randi Reisfeld	2001–2004		2005	Disney–ABC Domestic Television	Paranormal
The Chronicles of Narnia series	C. S. Lewis	1949–1954		2005–2010	Walden Media	High Fantasy
Eragon	Christopher Paolini	2002		2006	Davis Entertainment	High Fantasy
Aquamarine	Alice Hoffman	2001		2006	Storefront Pictures	Fantasy, Romance
Hoot	Carl Hiaasen	2002		2006	Walden Media; Kennedy/Marshall	Drama
The Thief Lord	Cornelia Funke	2000		2006	Warner Bros. Pictures (International); 20th Century Fox (North America)	Fantasy, adventure

BOOK (SERIES) TITLE	AUTHOR	YEAR OF PUBLICATION	FILM TITLE	YEAR OF RELEASE	MOVIE STUDIO	SUBGENRE
Stormbreaker (Alex Rider series)	Anthony Horowitz	2000	*Stormbreaker*	2006	The Weinstein Company; Moving Picture Company (MPC); Isle of Man Film; Samuelson Productions	Adventure, thriller, spy
The Golden Compass	Philip Pullman	1995		2007	New Line Cinema; Ingenious Film Partners; Scholastic Productions; Depth of Field; Rhythm and Hues	Dark fantasy
Blood and Chocolate	Annette Curtis Klause	1997		2007	Lakeshore Entertainment	Paranormal, Romance
Stardust	Neil Gaiman	1999		2007	Marv Films; Ingenious Film Partners	Fantasy, romance
The Dark Is Rising Sequence series	Susan Cooper	1984	*The Seeker: The Dark Is Rising*	2007	Walden Media	Fantasy
Alice series	Phyllis Reynolds Naylor	1985–2013	*Alice Upside Down*	2007	Open Pictures	Drama
Gossip Girl	Cecily von Ziegesar	2002–2011	(TV series)	2007–2012	Warner Bros. Television; CBS Television Studios; Fake Empire Productions; Alloy Entertainment; College Hill Pictures, Inc.	Chick lit
Angus, Thongs and Full Frontal Snogging/ It's Okay, I'm Wearing Really Big Knickers	Louise Rennison	1999/2000	*Angus, Thongs and Perfect Snogging*	2008	Nickelodeon Movies	Chick lit

BOOK (SERIES) TITLE	AUTHOR	YEAR OF PUBLICATION	FILM TITLE	YEAR OF RELEASE	MOVIE STUDIO	SUBGENRE
The Spiderwick Chronicles	Tony DiTerlizzi and Holly Blac	2003		2008	Nickelodeon Movies; Kennedy/ Marshall	Fantasy
City of Ember	Jeanne DuPrau	2003		2008	Walden Media; Playtone	Post-apocalyptic, science fiction
Nick and Norah's Infinite Playlist	Rachel Cohn, David Levithan	2008		2008	Mandate Pictures	Romance
Jumper	Steven Gould	1992		2008	Regency Enterprises; New Regency Productions	Science fiction
The Clique	Lisi Harrison	2004		2008	Alloy Entertainment; Bankable Productions	Chick lit
The Boy in the Striped Pajamas	John Boyne	2006		2008	BBC Films; Heyday Films	Historical, postmodern
Twilight series	Stephenie Meyer	2005–2008		2008–2012	Summit Entertainment	Paranormal, Romance
Youth in Revolt	C. D. Payne	1993		2009	Permut	Humor, romance
Coraline	Neil Gaiman	2002		2009	Laika; Pandemonium	Fantasy/ horror
The Lovely Bones	Alice Sebold	2002		2009	Film4 Productions; WingNut Films	Fantasy, drama
Inkheart	Cornelia Funke	2003		2009	New Line Cinema	Fantasy
Cirque du Freak: The Vampire's Assistant	Darren Shan	2000		2009	Relativity Media; The Donners' Company; Depth of Field	Paranormal
The Secret Dreamworld of a Shopaholic	Sophie Kinsella	2000	*Confessions of a Shopaholic*	2009	Touchstone Pictures; Jerry Bruckheimer Films	Chick lit

BOOK (SERIES) TITLE	AUTHOR	YEAR OF PUBLICATION	FILM TITLE	YEAR OF RELEASE	MOVIE STUDIO	SUBGENRE
I Love You Beth Cooper	Larry Doyle	2007		2009	1492 Pictures; The Bridge Studios; Ingenious Film Partners	Comedy, romance
Derby Girl	Shauna Cross	2007	*Whip It*	2009	Mandate Pictures; Flower Films	Drama
Vampire Diaries series	L. G. Smith, Aubrey Clark	1991–present	(TV series)	2009–present	Outerbanks Entertainment; Alloy Entertainment; CBS Television Studios; Warner Bros. Television	Paranormal, Romance
Flipped	Wendelin Van Draanen	2001		2010	Castle Rock Entertainment	Romance
Memoirs of a Teenage Amnesiac	Gabrielle Zevin	2009		2010	Aoi Production; Dot Dot Dot Films	Chick lit
It's Kind of a Funny Story	Ned Vizzini	2006		2010	Alliance Films; Misher Films; Wayfare Entertainment	Drama, humor, romance
Guardians of Ga'Hoole series	Kathryn Lasky	2003	*Legend of the Guardians: The Owls of Ga'Hoole*	2010	Village Roadshow Pictures; Animal Logic	High fantasy, animal adventure
Tomorrow, When the War Began	John Marsden	1993		2010	Ambience Entertainment; Omnilab Media	Adventure, thriller
Avalon High	Meg Cabot	2005		2010	Sudden Motion Productions; Ranger Productions	Mystery, fantasy
Percy Jackson series	Rick Riordan	2005–2009		2010–2013	1492 Pictures; Sunswept Entertainment	Fantasy

BOOK (SERIES) TITLE	AUTHOR	YEAR OF PUBLICATION	FILM TITLE	YEAR OF RELEASE	MOVIE STUDIO	SUBGENRE
Pretty Little Liars	Sara Shepard	2006–present	(TV series)	2010–present	Warner Horizon Television; Alloy Entertainment; Long Lake Productions; Russian Hill Productions	Mystery, thriller, drama
The Invention of Hugo Cabret	Brian Selznick	2007	*Hugo*	2011	GK Films and Infinitium Nihil	Historical
War Horse	Michael Morpurgo	1982		2011	Amblin Entertainment; The Kennedy/Marshall Company; DreamWorks Studios; Reliance Entertainment	Historical
Beastly	Alex Flinn	2007		2011	CBS Films; Alliance Films	Fantasy, Romance
I Am Number Four	Pittacus Lore	2010		2011	Touchstone Pictures; DreamWorks Studios; Reliance Big Entertainment; Bay Films	Science fiction, romance
Soul Surfer: A True Story of Faith, Family, and Fighting to Get Back on the Board	Bethany Hamilton	2004	*Soul Surfer*	2011	Mandalay Pictures; Brookwell McNamara Entertainment; Island Film Group; Enticing Entertainment; Affirm Films; Life's a Beach Entertainment	Drama
Jeremy Fink and the Meaning of Life	Wendy Mass	2006		2011	Fink Films; Kidzhouse Entertainment	Drama, mystery
Lemonade Mouth	Mark Peter Hughes	2007		2011	Martin Chase Productions; G Wave Productions	Drama

BOOK (SERIES) TITLE	AUTHOR	YEAR OF PUBLICATION	FILM TITLE	YEAR OF RELEASE	MOVIE STUDIO	SUBGENRE
The Secret Circle	L. G. Smith, Aubrey Clark	1992–present	(TV series)	2011–2012	Warner Bros. Television; CBS Television Studios; Alloy Entertainment; Outerbanks Entertainment	Fantasy, romance
The Perks of Being a Wallflower	Stephen Chbosky	1999		2012	Mr. Mudd	Drama
Before I Die	Jenny Downham	2007	Now Is Good	2012	Maverick Films	Drama
Tiger Eyes	Judy Blume	1981		2012	Tashmoo Production, Amber Entertainment	Drama
Someday This Pain Will Be Useful to You	Peter Cameron	2007		2012	Jean Vigo Italia Four of a Kind Productions	Drama, humor
The Hunger Games series	Suzanne Collins	2008/2009/2010		2012–	Color Force	Dystopian
Beautiful Creatures	Kami Garcia and Margaret Stohl	2009		2013	Alcon Entertainment	Fantasy/Romance
The Host	Stephanie Meyer	2008		2013	Nick Wechsler Productions; Silver Reel	Scifi/Romance
The Mortal Instruments: City of Bones	Cassandra Clare	2007		2013	Constantin Film Produktion; Sony Pictures Entertainment; Unique Features	Urban fantasy
The Spectacular Now	Tim Tharp	2008		2013	21 Laps Entertainment	Drama, romance
Ender's Game	Orson Scott Card	1985		2013	Chartoff Productions Taleswapper OddLot Entertainment K/O Paper Products Digital Domain	Science Fiction

BOOK (SERIES) TITLE	AUTHOR	YEAR OF PUBLICATION	FILM TITLE	YEAR OF RELEASE	MOVIE STUDIO	SUBGENRE
The Hundred	Kass Morgan	2013	(TV series)	2013	Bonanza Productions; Alloy Entertainment (in association with) Warner Bros. Television (in association with) CBS Television Studios	Dystopian
The Book Thief	Markus Zuzak	2006		2013	Babelsberg Studios	Historical
Vampire Acadamy	Richelle Mead	2007	Vampire Academy: Blood Sisters	2014	Preger Entertainment; Kintop Pictures/ Reliance; Angry Films	Paranormal, Romance, Urban Fantasy
Maze Runner	James Dashner	2009		2014	20th Century Fox	Dystopian, Science fiction
Divergent	Veronica Roth	2011		2014	Summit Entertainment; Red Wagon Entertainment	Dystopian, Romance
Fault in Our Stars	John Green	2012		2014	20th Century Fox	Romance
The Giver	Lois Lowry	1993		2014	The Weinstein Company	Dystopian, science fiction
The Spook's Apprentice	Joseph Delaney	2004	Seventh Son	2015	Legendary Pictures	High Fantasy

*Note: Many movies and books prior to 2000 may have not been categorized as young adult, but today might be.

APPENDIX E

Young Adult Publishers

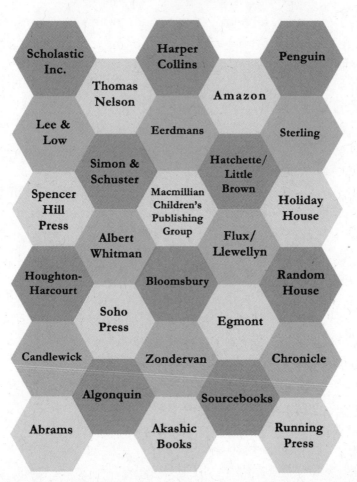

Scholastic Inc.

Harper Collins

Penguin

Thomas Nelson

Amazon

Lee & Low

Eerdmans

Sterling

Simon & Schuster

Hatchette/ Little Brown

Spencer Hill Press

Macmillian Children's Publishing Group

Holiday House

Albert Whitman

Flux/ Llewellyn

Houghton-Harcourt

Bloomsbury

Random House

Soho Press

Egmont

Candlewick

Zondervan

Chronicle

Algonquin

Sourcebooks

Abrams

Akashic Books

Running Press

ACKNOWLEDGMENTS

To all educators, MFA programs, writers groups, librarians, and bloggers, and to everyone who has told me that they are using *Writing Great Books for Young Adults* in their writing classes. Thank you so much for making the first edition so successful. I'm collecting a list of adopters of the book. Please let me know who you are.

If you'd like me to come and speak to your group or class, I'd love to. I encourage you to reach out to me at rbrooks@serendipitylit. com, at www.serendipitylit.com, or on Twitter at @serendipitylit.

To Katharine Sands, the true example of the universes promise to offer a guiding voice. Your irrepressible excitement is always the burst to get me moving, and *always* in the right direction.

Anne Wells, you are my fortifier. Thank you for always being there when I need help in finding my voice. You are an editor extraordinaire. May this open the door to many more bestsellers.

To Benjamin Haberman and Emily Becker, my dedicated research team, thanks for your probing and for finding precise facts.

To Samantha Schechter, thanks for your illustrative renderings.

Stephanie Bowen and Jenna Skwarek, much appreciation for your role in reinvigorating the book. Thank you for acquiring and developing a plan for the second edition and helping me celebrate the new and wonderful world of YA.

Thanks to all the editors and publishing professionals who contributed their expertise in this second edition. We can all be proud to have played a pivotal role in educating a new school of young adult writers.

To Xander, who encourages me and always points me to see the land beyond the horizon. Your friendship and advice are invaluable.

Thank you to all the bloggers who have supported the Serendipity YA Discovery Contest for the last five years. The contest has opened the way for many debut writers to get a leg up in the industry. Thank you Paul Samuelson, my first Sourcebooks publicist, for knowing exactly how to get audiences engaged.

A special thanks to my able and dedicated collaborators, to my proofreader, Sharon Sofinski, publicist, Katy Lynch, production editor, Rachel Kahn, designer, Jillian Rahn, and to Marketing.

Dear Reader: Let me hear from you! And remember, one of the best things you can do for an author is to write a positive review. I encourage you to do so through Goodreads, Amazon, or your point-of-purchase location or via email at rbrooks@serendipitylit.com.

FROM THE FIRST EDITION

My deepest gratitude goes to the inspirational Katharine Sands, my soul sister, without whose coaxing and unyielding enthusiasm this book never would have been written. I'm forever thankful to you for seeing a light in me.

To my exceptional editorial and writing guides, John Weber, whose generosity and exceptional eye for excellence has brought me an abundance of everything good; and my editorial carpenter, Brenda Richardson, who can bring shape to nearly anything. Anne Wells, you're always there when I need you with incomparable editorial guidance.

To Serendipity Literary Agency staff who researched and edited for me: Debarati Sengupta, Meeta Atul Pingle, Megan Ernst, and James Seraphin.

To Sherrie Young, my partner in YB Literary Foundation whose visionary ideas always keep me assured I'm on the right track; your opinion and feedback are like magic dust.

Special thanks to Dauwd Ruffin, who at a moment's notice had an answer. Having your brilliance near me and your unending support makes me feel truly blessed!

To Flora Anders, whose motivation and support early on prepared me for the publishing industry as she watched over my career and nurtured me like a surrogate mom.

To all my friends who cheered me on through the demanding writing stages.

I wish to thank the numerous people who really helped make this book a reality, including those who filled out surveys and agreed to be interviewed, and those who shared their knowledge anecdotally and whose contributions you'll see sprinkled through the text.

A million thanks to Peter Lynch, my editor, who had the insight to see the book's potential. I am forever thankful for your relentless patience and editorial acumen.

To my copy editor Claire Martinson, thanks for dotting the i's and crossing the t's. After having worked on the manuscript for months, having your eyes were priceless.

To the team at Sourcebooks, who just seem to get it.

INDEX

ABOUT THE AUTHOR

Regina L. Brooks is the president and CEO of Serendipity Literary Agency LLC, based in New York, New York. She represents a diverse base of award-winning clients in adult and young adult fiction, nonfiction, and children's literature, including: three-time National Book Award finalist, Newbery Honor Winner, and the Coretta Scott King Honor and the 2006 Michael Printz Honor Award–winning author Marilyn Nelson; winner of the Coretta Scott King/John Steptoe New Talent Award, Al Roker's Book Club for Kids author Sundee Frazier; and Stonewall and Lambda Book Award winner, Bil Wright. She is the author of several books including *Never Finished, Never Done!* (Scholastic), *Writing Great Books for Young Adults* (Sourcebooks), and *You Should Really Write a Book: How to Write, Sell, and Market Your Memoir* (St. Martin's Press), as well as a blogger for the *Huffington Post*. Brooks is on the faculty of the Writer's Digest University, Harvard University publishing course, the Discovery Channel's Media Boot Camp for Doctors, and the Whidbey Island Writers MFA program, and teaches annually at more than twenty international conferences. She has been highlighted in several national and international magazines and periodicals, including *Forbes*, *Media Bistro*, *Writers and Poets*, *Essence Magazine*, *Ebony*, *Jet*, *Women on Writing*, *Writers Digest Magazine*, and the *Writer*. She is a member of the Association of Author Representatives and is on the board of several literary organizations including Grub Street. She has served as a judge for the NAACP Image Awards. Ms. Brooks is the founder and co-executive director of YB Literary Foundation, Inc., a not-for-profit organization for teens, designed to kindle a passion for literature and an appreciation for the possibilities and opportunities that being a developed reader can provide (www.ybliterary.org). She is always interested in new and emerging writers visit (www .serendipitylit.com). When she's not reading or helping authors, she takes to the sky with her flying club, Brooklyn Aviation.